75 Japanese Inspired Recipes for Home

By: Kelly Johnson

Table of Contents

Recipes

- Teriyaki Glazed Salmon with Sesame Ginger Quinoa
- Miso Maple Glazed Eggplant with Soba Noodles
- Tempura Vegetable Udon Noodle Bowl
- Gyoza with Ponzu Dipping Sauce
- Sushi Bowl with Teriyaki Tofu and Avocado
- Yaki Udon with Mixed Vegetables and Tofu
- Matcha Green Tea Tiramisu
- Okonomiyaki - Japanese Savory Pancake
- Japanese-Inspired Miso Ramen Bowl
- Japanese-Inspired Teriyaki Chicken Donburi
- Japanese Matcha Cheesecake Bars
- Japanese-Inspired Kinako Mochi Ice Cream
- Japanese-Inspired Chirashi Sushi Bowl
- **Japanese-Inspired Sesame Teriyaki Chicken Skewers**
- **Japanese Sweet Potato Korokke (Croquettes)**
- Japanese-Inspired Nasu Dengaku (Miso-Glazed Eggplant)
- Japanese-Inspired Sakura Mochi
- Japanese Hōtō Nabe (Flat Udon Noodle Hot Pot)
- Japanese-Inspired Tamago Sando (Egg Sandwich)
- Japanese-Inspired Gyoza Dumplings
- Japanese-Inspired Katsudon (Pork Cutlet Rice Bowl)
- Japanese-Inspired Teriyaki Salmon Bowl
- Japanese-Inspired Shrimp Tempura Udon
- Japanese-Inspired Matcha Latte
- Japanese-Inspired Okonomiyaki (Cabbage Pancake)
- Japanese-Inspired Yaki Udon (Stir-Fried Udon Noodles)
- Sakura Sizzle Stir-Fry
- Miso Glazed Salmon with Wasabi Mash
- Teriyaki Tofu and Vegetable Soba Noodles
- Matcha Green Tea Cheesecake
- Okonomiyaki - Japanese Savory Pancake
- Gyoza - Japanese Pan-Fried Dumplings
- Chawanmushi - Japanese Steamed Egg Custard
- Nikujaga - Japanese Meat and Potato Stew

- Katsudon - Japanese Pork Cutlet Bowl
- Yaki Udon - Japanese Stir-Fried Udon Noodles
- **Sunomono - Japanese Cucumber Salad**

- Tamago Sushi - Japanese Sweet Rolled Omelette Sushi
- Hōtō Nabe - Japanese Pumpkin and Noodle Hot Pot
- Gyudon - Japanese Beef Bowl
- Ebi Chili - Japanese Spicy Chili Shrimp
- Chirashi Sushi - Japanese Scattered Sushi Bowl
- Okonomiyaki - Japanese Savory Pancake
- Miso Soup with Tofu and Wakame
- Hiyashi Chuka - Japanese Cold Ramen Salad
- Yakitori - Japanese Grilled Chicken Skewers
- Nikujaga - Japanese Meat and Potato Stew
- **Katsudon - Japanese Pork Cutlet Bowl**

- Gomae - Japanese Spinach Salad with Sesame Dressing
- Yaki Udon - Japanese Stir-Fried Udon Noodles
- **Chawanmushi - Japanese Steamed Egg Custard**

- Sunomono - Japanese Cucumber Salad
- Dorayaki - Japanese Red Bean Pancake Sandwiches
- Oyakodon - Japanese Chicken and Egg Rice Bowl
- Gyu Don - Japanese Beef Bowl
- Tamago Sando - Japanese Egg Salad Sandwich
- Hōtō - Japanese Pumpkin and Noodle Stew
- **Okonomiyaki - Japanese Savory Pancake**

- Zaru Soba - Japanese Cold Buckwheat Noodles
- Miso Soup with Tofu and Wakame
- Nikujaga - Japanese Meat and Potato Stew
- Goma-ae - Japanese Sesame Spinach Salad
- Ebi Chili - Japanese Spicy Chili Prawns

- Chawanmushi - Japanese Steamed Egg Custard
- **Buta Kakuni - Japanese Braised Pork Belly**

- Nasu Dengaku - Japanese Miso-Glazed Eggplant
- Yudofu - Japanese Hot Tofu Soup
- Unagi Don - Japanese Grilled Eel Rice Bowl
- Dorayaki - Japanese Red Bean Pancake Sandwiches
- Takoyaki - Japanese Octopus Balls
- Okonomiyaki - Japanese Savory Pancake

- Sakura Soba Noodles with Tempura Vegetables
- Miso Glazed Grilled Salmon with Sake-infused Jasmine Rice
- Teriyaki Tofu Stir-Fry with Udon Noodles
- Matcha Green Tea Pancakes with Red Bean Paste Drizzle

Teriyaki Glazed Salmon with Sesame Ginger Quinoa

Ingredients:

For the Teriyaki Glazed Salmon:

- 4 salmon fillets
- 1/4 cup soy sauce
- 2 tablespoons mirin
- 2 tablespoons sake
- 2 tablespoons brown sugar
- 1 tablespoon grated fresh ginger
- 2 cloves garlic, minced
- 1 tablespoon sesame oil
- Sesame seeds for garnish

For the Sesame Ginger Quinoa:

- 1 cup quinoa, rinsed
- 2 cups water
- 1 tablespoon sesame oil
- 2 tablespoons soy sauce
- 1 tablespoon rice vinegar
- 1 tablespoon fresh ginger, finely grated
- 2 green onions, thinly sliced
- 1 tablespoon toasted sesame seeds

Instructions:

In a small saucepan, combine soy sauce, mirin, sake, brown sugar, grated ginger, minced garlic, and sesame oil for the teriyaki glaze. Heat over medium-low heat until the sugar dissolves and the sauce thickens slightly. Set aside.
Preheat the oven to 400°F (200°C).
Place the salmon fillets on a baking sheet lined with parchment paper. Brush the teriyaki glaze generously over each fillet, reserving some for basting.
Bake the salmon in the preheated oven for about 15-20 minutes, or until the salmon is cooked through and flakes easily. Baste the salmon with the teriyaki glaze halfway through the cooking time.

While the salmon is baking, prepare the sesame ginger quinoa. In a medium saucepan, combine quinoa and water. Bring to a boil, then reduce heat to low, cover, and simmer for 15 minutes, or until the quinoa is cooked and water is absorbed.

In a small bowl, whisk together sesame oil, soy sauce, rice vinegar, and grated ginger. Fluff the cooked quinoa with a fork and drizzle the dressing over it. Stir in sliced green onions and sprinkle toasted sesame seeds on top.

Serve the teriyaki glazed salmon fillets over a bed of sesame ginger quinoa. Garnish with additional sesame seeds and chopped green onions.

This Japanese-inspired dish combines the sweet and savory flavors of teriyaki-glazed salmon with the nutty and aromatic sesame ginger quinoa, creating a delightful and wholesome meal.

Miso Maple Glazed Eggplant with Soba Noodles

Ingredients:

For the Miso Maple Glazed Eggplant:

- 2 large Japanese eggplants, sliced
- 3 tablespoons white miso paste
- 2 tablespoons maple syrup
- 2 tablespoons rice vinegar
- 2 tablespoons soy sauce
- 1 tablespoon sesame oil
- 2 cloves garlic, minced
- 1 teaspoon grated fresh ginger
- Sesame seeds and sliced green onions for garnish

For the Soba Noodles:

- 8 oz (about 225g) soba noodles
- 1 tablespoon soy sauce
- 1 tablespoon sesame oil
- 1 tablespoon rice vinegar
- 1 teaspoon honey
- 1 teaspoon toasted sesame seeds

Instructions:

Preheat the oven to 400°F (200°C).
In a bowl, whisk together miso paste, maple syrup, rice vinegar, soy sauce, sesame oil, minced garlic, and grated ginger to create the miso maple glaze.
Place the sliced eggplants on a baking sheet lined with parchment paper. Brush the miso maple glaze over each slice, ensuring they are well-coated.
Roast the glazed eggplant slices in the preheated oven for 20-25 minutes or until they are golden brown and tender. Flip the slices halfway through the cooking time and baste with additional glaze.
While the eggplant is roasting, cook the soba noodles according to package instructions. Drain and rinse under cold water.
In a small bowl, mix soy sauce, sesame oil, rice vinegar, honey, and toasted sesame seeds for the soba noodle dressing.

Toss the cooked soba noodles in the dressing until well-coated.
Serve the miso maple glazed eggplant slices on a bed of soba noodles. Garnish with sesame seeds and sliced green onions.

This Japanese-inspired dish features the rich umami flavors of miso and the sweetness of maple glazed over roasted eggplant, paired with the delightful texture of soba noodles for a satisfying and flavorful meal.

Tempura Vegetable Udon Noodle Bowl

Ingredients:

For the Tempura Vegetables:

- Assorted vegetables (e.g., sweet potatoes, bell peppers, zucchini, mushrooms)
- 1 cup all-purpose flour
- 1 cup ice-cold sparkling water
- Vegetable oil for frying
- Salt for seasoning

For the Udon Noodle Bowl:

- 8 oz (about 225g) udon noodles
- 4 cups vegetable broth
- 3 tablespoons soy sauce
- 1 tablespoon mirin
- 1 tablespoon sake (optional)
- 1 tablespoon sesame oil
- 1 tablespoon grated daikon radish (for garnish)
- Chopped green onions for garnish

Instructions:

Prepare the tempura batter by whisking together all-purpose flour and ice-cold sparkling water until you achieve a smooth consistency. The batter should be slightly lumpy.
Cut the assorted vegetables into bite-sized pieces suitable for tempura.
Heat vegetable oil in a deep fryer or a large, deep pan to 350°F (175°C).
Dip the vegetable pieces into the tempura batter, coating them evenly.
Carefully place the battered vegetables into the hot oil and fry until golden brown and crispy. Remove with a slotted spoon and place them on a paper towel-lined plate. Sprinkle with salt while still hot.
Cook udon noodles according to package instructions. Drain and set aside.
In a separate pot, heat vegetable broth, soy sauce, mirin, sake (if using), and sesame oil. Bring to a simmer.
Divide the cooked udon noodles among serving bowls. Pour the hot broth over the noodles.

Arrange the tempura vegetables on top of the udon noodles.
Garnish with grated daikon radish and chopped green onions.

Serve this Tempura Vegetable Udon Noodle Bowl for a Japanese-inspired dish that combines the crispy goodness of tempura vegetables with the comforting warmth of udon noodles in a flavorful broth.

Gyoza with Ponzu Dipping Sauce

Ingredients:

For the Gyoza Filling:

- 1/2 pound (about 225g) ground pork
- 1 cup napa cabbage, finely chopped
- 2 green onions, finely chopped
- 2 cloves garlic, minced
- 1 tablespoon soy sauce
- 1 tablespoon sesame oil
- 1 teaspoon fresh ginger, grated
- 1/2 teaspoon sugar
- 1/2 teaspoon black pepper
- Gyoza wrappers

For the Ponzu Dipping Sauce:

- 1/4 cup soy sauce
- 2 tablespoons rice vinegar
- 1 tablespoon fresh lime juice
- 1 tablespoon mirin
- 1 teaspoon soy sauce
- 1 teaspoon honey
- 1 teaspoon grated daikon radish (optional)
- Thinly sliced green onions for garnish

Instructions:

In a bowl, combine ground pork, chopped napa cabbage, green onions, minced garlic, soy sauce, sesame oil, grated ginger, sugar, and black pepper. Mix well to create the gyoza filling.

Place a small amount of the filling in the center of a gyoza wrapper. Moisten the edges of the wrapper with water and fold it in half, pleating the edges to seal. Repeat with the remaining filling and wrappers.

Heat a skillet over medium-high heat and add a small amount of oil. Place the gyoza in the skillet and cook until the bottoms are golden brown.

Once the bottoms are browned, add water to the skillet (enough to cover the bottom) and cover with a lid. Steam the gyoza for 5-7 minutes or until the pork is cooked through.

While the gyoza is cooking, prepare the ponzu dipping sauce by combining soy sauce, rice vinegar, fresh lime juice, mirin, soy sauce, honey, and grated daikon radish (if using).

Remove the lid from the skillet and let the gyoza cook uncovered for an additional 2-3 minutes, allowing the bottoms to crisp up again.

Serve the gyoza hot with the ponzu dipping sauce. Garnish with thinly sliced green onions.

Enjoy these delicious Gyoza with Ponzu Dipping Sauce as a Japanese-inspired appetizer or part of a meal. The combination of savory pork filling and tangy ponzu sauce creates a delightful taste experience.

Sushi Bowl with Teriyaki Tofu and Avocado

Ingredients:

For the Teriyaki Tofu:

- 1 block extra-firm tofu, pressed and cubed
- 3 tablespoons soy sauce
- 2 tablespoons mirin
- 1 tablespoon maple syrup
- 1 tablespoon sesame oil
- 1 teaspoon grated fresh ginger
- 1 clove garlic, minced

For the Sushi Bowl:

- 2 cups sushi rice, cooked and seasoned with rice vinegar
- 1 avocado, sliced
- 1 cucumber, julienned
- 1 carrot, julienned
- 1 nori sheet, thinly sliced
- Sesame seeds for garnish
- Pickled ginger and soy sauce for serving

Instructions:

In a bowl, whisk together soy sauce, mirin, maple syrup, sesame oil, grated ginger, and minced garlic for the teriyaki marinade.
Place the cubed tofu in a shallow dish and pour the teriyaki marinade over it.
Allow the tofu to marinate for at least 30 minutes.
Heat a skillet over medium heat and add the marinated tofu cubes. Cook until the tofu is golden brown on all sides, absorbing the teriyaki flavors. Set aside.
Assemble the sushi bowl by placing a serving of seasoned sushi rice in each bowl.
Arrange teriyaki tofu cubes, sliced avocado, julienned cucumber, and julienned carrot on top of the rice.
Sprinkle sliced nori and sesame seeds over the bowl for added flavor and texture.
Serve the sushi bowl with pickled ginger on the side and a small bowl of soy sauce for dipping.

This Sushi Bowl with Teriyaki Tofu and Avocado provides all the flavors of sushi in a convenient bowl format. The combination of teriyaki-marinated tofu, fresh vegetables, and creamy avocado makes for a delicious and satisfying meal.

Yaki Udon with Mixed Vegetables and Tofu

Ingredients:

For the Yaki Udon:

- 8 oz (about 225g) udon noodles, cooked and drained
- 1 block firm tofu, pressed and cubed
- 2 tablespoons vegetable oil
- 1 onion, thinly sliced
- 2 carrots, julienned
- 1 bell pepper, thinly sliced
- 01 cup broccoli florets
- 2 cups cabbage, thinly sliced
- 3 cloves garlic, minced
- 1/4 cup soy sauce
- 2 tablespoons mirin
- 1 tablespoon sake (optional)
- 1 tablespoon oyster sauce
- 1 tablespoon sesame oil
- 1 tablespoon brown sugar
- Sesame seeds and chopped green onions for garnish

Instructions:

In a wok or large skillet, heat vegetable oil over medium-high heat. Add the cubed tofu and stir-fry until golden brown. Remove tofu from the pan and set aside.
In the same pan, add a bit more oil if needed. Add sliced onion, julienned carrots, bell pepper, broccoli florets, cabbage, and minced garlic. Stir-fry for 3-5 minutes or until the vegetables are tender-crisp.
Add the cooked udon noodles to the vegetables and toss to combine.
In a small bowl, mix together soy sauce, mirin, sake (if using), oyster sauce, sesame oil, and brown sugar. Pour the sauce over the udon and vegetables. Toss everything together to ensure even coating.
Add the cooked tofu back into the pan and gently stir to incorporate.
Cook for an additional 2-3 minutes, allowing the flavors to meld and the dish to heat through.
Serve the Yaki Udon hot, garnished with sesame seeds and chopped green onions.

This Yaki Udon with Mixed Vegetables and Tofu offers a delightful stir-fried noodle dish with a medley of colorful vegetables, tofu, and a savory-sweet sauce, providing a satisfying and flavorful Japanese-inspired meal.

Matcha Green Tea Tiramisu

Ingredients:

For the Matcha Mascarpone Mixture:

- 1 cup mascarpone cheese
- 1/2 cup powdered sugar
- 2 tablespoons matcha powder
- 1 teaspoon vanilla extract

For the Soaking Syrup:

- 1 cup strong brewed green tea, cooled
- 2 tablespoons honey
- 1 tablespoon matcha powder

For Assembly:

- Ladyfinger cookies
- Unsweetened cocoa powder for dusting
- Matcha powder for dusting

Instructions:

In a bowl, whisk together mascarpone cheese, powdered sugar, matcha powder, and vanilla extract until smooth and well combined. Set aside.
In a separate bowl, mix together brewed green tea, honey, and matcha powder to create the soaking syrup. Ensure the matcha powder is fully dissolved.
Dip ladyfinger cookies into the matcha soaking syrup, making sure to coat them evenly. Arrange a layer of soaked ladyfingers in the bottom of a serving dish.
Spread a portion of the matcha mascarpone mixture over the layer of ladyfingers. Repeat the process, creating alternating layers of soaked ladyfingers and matcha mascarpone mixture until you reach the top of the serving dish, finishing with a layer of the mascarpone mixture on top.
Cover the dish with plastic wrap and refrigerate for at least 4 hours or overnight to allow the flavors to meld and the tiramisu to set.
Before serving, dust the top of the tiramisu with unsweetened cocoa powder and matcha powder for an elegant finish.
Slice and serve the Matcha Green Tea Tiramisu chilled.

This Matcha Green Tea Tiramisu offers a unique twist on the classic Italian dessert, infusing it with the earthy and vibrant flavors of matcha for a delightful and visually stunning treat.

Okonomiyaki - Japanese Savory Pancake

Ingredients:

For the Okonomiyaki Batter:

- 2 cups shredded cabbage
- 1 cup all-purpose flour
- 1 cup dashi stock (or water)
- 2 large eggs
- 1 tablespoon soy sauce
- 1 teaspoon baking powder
- Salt and pepper to taste

For the Okonomiyaki Fillings (choose your favorites):

- 1 cup cooked and chopped shrimp
- 1 cup thinly sliced pork belly or bacon
- 1 cup chopped scallions
- 1/2 cup pickled red ginger (beni shoga)
- 1/2 cup tenkasu (tempura scraps)

For Toppings:

- Okonomiyaki sauce
- Japanese mayonnaise
- Bonito flakes (katsuobushi)
- Aonori (dried seaweed flakes)

Instructions:

In a large bowl, combine shredded cabbage, all-purpose flour, dashi stock (or water), eggs, soy sauce, baking powder, salt, and pepper. Mix until well combined to create the okonomiyaki batter.
Add your choice of fillings to the batter. Common variations include shrimp, pork belly, scallions, pickled red ginger, and tenkasu.
Heat a griddle or non-stick skillet over medium heat. Grease the surface lightly with oil.

Pour a portion of the batter onto the griddle, spreading it into a round pancake shape. Cook for 4-5 minutes on each side or until golden brown and cooked through.

Repeat the process for the remaining batter, creating multiple okonomiyaki pancakes.

Once cooked, drizzle okonomiyaki sauce and Japanese mayonnaise over the top of each pancake.

Sprinkle bonito flakes and aonori on top for added flavor and texture.

Slice the okonomiyaki into wedges and serve hot.

Enjoy this Okonomiyaki – a delicious Japanese savory pancake that allows for creativity with fillings and toppings, providing a tasty and satisfying meal.

Japanese-Inspired Miso Ramen Bowl

Ingredients:

For the Miso Broth:

- 4 cups vegetable broth
- 3 tablespoons white miso paste
- 2 tablespoons soy sauce
- 1 tablespoon sesame oil
- 1 tablespoon mirin
- 1 tablespoon grated fresh ginger
- 2 cloves garlic, minced

For the Ramen Bowl:

- 8 oz (about 225g) ramen noodles
- 1 cup sliced shiitake mushrooms
- 1 cup baby bok choy, chopped
- 1 cup tofu cubes, pressed
- 1 cup bean sprouts
- 2 green onions, thinly sliced
- Nori sheets, sliced for garnish
- Sesame seeds for garnish

Optional Toppings:

- Soft-boiled eggs
- Sriracha sauce

Instructions:

In a pot, combine vegetable broth, white miso paste, soy sauce, sesame oil, mirin, grated ginger, and minced garlic for the miso broth. Bring to a simmer and let it simmer for 10-15 minutes to allow the flavors to meld.
Cook the ramen noodles according to package instructions. Drain and set aside. In a separate pan, sauté sliced shiitake mushrooms until tender. Add baby bok choy and tofu cubes, cooking until bok choy is wilted, and tofu is golden brown. Divide the cooked ramen noodles among serving bowls. Ladle the miso broth over the noodles.

Arrange the sautéed mushrooms, bok choy, tofu cubes, bean sprouts, and sliced green onions on top of the noodles.
Garnish with nori slices and sesame seeds.
Optional: Top each bowl with a soft-boiled egg and drizzle with sriracha sauce for added flavor and spice.
Serve the Japanese-Inspired Miso Ramen Bowl hot.

This Miso Ramen Bowl combines the umami-rich flavors of miso with a variety of fresh and wholesome ingredients, creating a comforting and satisfying Japanese-inspired noodle dish.

Japanese-Inspired Teriyaki Chicken Donburi

Ingredients:

For the Teriyaki Chicken:

- 1 lb (about 450g) boneless, skinless chicken thighs, thinly sliced
- 1/4 cup soy sauce
- 2 tablespoons mirin
- 1 tablespoon sake (optional)
- 1 tablespoon honey
- 1 tablespoon sesame oil
- 2 cloves garlic, minced
- 1 teaspoon grated fresh ginger

For the Donburi Bowl:

- 2 cups cooked Japanese short-grain rice
- 1 cup broccoli florets, steamed
- 1 carrot, julienned
- 1/2 cup edamame, shelled
- 2 green onions, thinly sliced
- Sesame seeds for garnish

Instructions:

In a bowl, mix together soy sauce, mirin, sake (if using), honey, sesame oil, minced garlic, and grated ginger to create the teriyaki marinade.

Place the thinly sliced chicken thighs in the marinade and let them marinate for at least 30 minutes.

Heat a skillet over medium-high heat and add a bit of oil. Cook the marinated chicken slices until fully cooked and caramelized.

While the chicken is cooking, prepare the donburi bowl components. Steam broccoli florets, julienne the carrot, and cook edamame according to package instructions.

Assemble the donburi bowls by placing a serving of cooked Japanese short-grain rice at the bottom of each bowl.

Arrange the teriyaki chicken slices on top of the rice.

Add steamed broccoli, julienned carrot, and edamame around the chicken.

Garnish with sliced green onions and sprinkle sesame seeds over the bowl.
Optional: Drizzle a little extra teriyaki sauce over the top for added flavor.
Serve the Japanese-Inspired Teriyaki Chicken Donburi hot.

This Teriyaki Chicken Donburi offers a delicious combination of savory teriyaki chicken, steamed vegetables, and fluffy rice in a bowl, creating a satisfying and flavorful Japanese-inspired meal.

Japanese Matcha Cheesecake Bars

Ingredients:

For the Matcha Cheesecake Layer:

- 2 cups cream cheese, softened
- 1/2 cup granulated sugar
- 2 tablespoons all-purpose flour
- 3 large eggs
- 1/2 cup sour cream
- 1 tablespoon matcha powder
- 1 teaspoon vanilla extract

For the Graham Cracker Crust:

- 1 1/2 cups graham cracker crumbs
- 1/4 cup unsalted butter, melted
- 2 tablespoons granulated sugar

For Topping:

- Whipped cream (optional)
- Matcha powder for dusting

Instructions:

Preheat the oven to 325°F (163°C). Line a square baking pan with parchment paper, leaving an overhang for easy removal.
In a bowl, combine graham cracker crumbs, melted butter, and sugar for the crust. Press the mixture into the bottom of the prepared pan to form an even layer.
In a large mixing bowl, beat cream cheese until smooth and creamy. Add sugar and flour, and beat until well combined.
Add eggs one at a time, beating well after each addition. Add sour cream, matcha powder, and vanilla extract. Mix until the batter is smooth and evenly colored.
Pour the matcha cheesecake batter over the graham cracker crust in the prepared pan.
Bake in the preheated oven for 30-35 minutes or until the edges are set, and the center is slightly jiggly.

Allow the cheesecake bars to cool completely in the pan. Once cooled, refrigerate for at least 4 hours or overnight to set.
Lift the cheesecake out of the pan using the parchment paper overhang. Cut into bars.
Optional: Before serving, top each bar with a dollop of whipped cream and dust with matcha powder.
Serve these Japanese Matcha Cheesecake Bars chilled.

These Matcha Cheesecake Bars offer a delightful combination of rich and creamy matcha-flavored cheesecake on a graham cracker crust, creating a delicious treat with a touch of Japanese flair.

Japanese-Inspired Kinako Mochi Ice Cream

Ingredients:

For the Mochi:

- 1 cup glutinous rice flour
- 1/4 cup sugar
- 3/4 cup water
- Potato starch or cornstarch for dusting

For the Kinako Coating:

- 1/2 cup kinako (roasted soybean flour)
- 1/4 cup powdered sugar

For Assembly:

- Your favorite ice cream (green tea, red bean, or vanilla work well)

Instructions:

In a heatproof bowl, whisk together glutinous rice flour, sugar, and water until smooth.
Cover the bowl loosely with plastic wrap and microwave on high for 2-3 minutes, stirring every minute, until the mixture becomes a thick, sticky dough.
Allow the mochi dough to cool slightly. While still warm, dust a clean surface with potato starch or cornstarch.
Transfer the mochi dough to the dusted surface and flatten it into a thin layer using a rolling pin or your hands.
Cut the mochi into squares, placing a small scoop of your favorite ice cream in the center of each square.
Gather the edges of the mochi around the ice cream, sealing it into a ball. Dust with more potato starch or cornstarch to prevent sticking.
In a separate bowl, mix kinako (roasted soybean flour) and powdered sugar to create the kinako coating.
Roll each mochi ice cream ball in the kinako coating until evenly covered.
Place the kinako-coated mochi ice cream balls on a tray lined with parchment paper and freeze for at least 2 hours or until firm.
Serve these delightful Kinako Mochi Ice Cream treats straight from the freezer.

These Japanese-inspired Kinako Mochi Ice Cream balls offer a chewy and sweet mochi exterior coated with the nutty flavor of kinako, providing a unique and delightful frozen treat.

Japanese-Inspired Chirashi Sushi Bowl

Ingredients:

For the Sushi Rice:

- 2 cups sushi rice
- 2 1/2 cups water
- 1/2 cup rice vinegar
- 3 tablespoons sugar
- 1 teaspoon salt

For the Chirashi Toppings:

- Assorted sashimi (salmon, tuna, shrimp, etc.), thinly sliced
- Tamago (sweet Japanese omelette), thinly sliced
- Avocado, sliced
- Radishes, thinly sliced
- Cucumber, julienned
- Pickled ginger
- Sesame seeds for garnish
- Nori strips for garnish

For the Soy Ginger Sauce:

- 1/4 cup soy sauce
- 1 tablespoon mirin
- 1 tablespoon rice vinegar
- 1 teaspoon grated fresh ginger
- 1 teaspoon sesame oil

Instructions:

Rinse sushi rice under cold water until the water runs clear. Cook the rice according to package instructions.
While the rice is still hot, mix rice vinegar, sugar, and salt. Gently fold the mixture into the cooked rice, fanning the rice to cool and achieve a glossy finish.
In a small bowl, whisk together soy sauce, mirin, rice vinegar, grated ginger, and sesame oil to create the soy ginger sauce. Set aside.

Assemble the chirashi sushi bowl by placing a generous portion of sushi rice in each serving bowl.
Arrange assorted sashimi, tamago slices, avocado, radishes, and julienned cucumber on top of the rice.
Drizzle the soy ginger sauce over the sushi bowl.
Garnish with pickled ginger, sesame seeds, and nori strips.
Serve the Japanese-Inspired Chirashi Sushi Bowl immediately.

This Chirashi Sushi Bowl offers a vibrant and visually appealing assortment of fresh sashimi, tamago, and vegetables over a bed of seasoned sushi rice, creating a delightful Japanese-inspired meal.

Japanese-Inspired Sesame Teriyaki Chicken Skewers

Ingredients:

For the Teriyaki Chicken Marinade:

- 1 lb (about 450g) boneless, skinless chicken thighs, cut into bite-sized pieces
- 1/4 cup soy sauce
- 2 tablespoons mirin
- 1 tablespoon sake (optional)
- 2 tablespoons honey
- 1 tablespoon sesame oil
- 2 cloves garlic, minced
- 1 teaspoon grated fresh ginger

For the Sesame Glaze:

- 2 tablespoons sesame seeds, toasted
- 1 tablespoon honey
- 1 tablespoon soy sauce

For Skewers:

- Bamboo skewers, soaked in water for at least 30 minutes

For Garnish:

- Chopped green onions
- Toasted sesame seeds

Instructions:

In a bowl, mix together soy sauce, mirin, sake (if using), honey, sesame oil, minced garlic, and grated ginger for the teriyaki marinade.
Add the bite-sized chicken pieces to the marinade, ensuring they are well-coated. Allow the chicken to marinate for at least 30 minutes.
While the chicken is marinating, preheat a grill or grill pan over medium-high heat.
Thread the marinated chicken pieces onto the soaked bamboo skewers.

Grill the chicken skewers for 8-10 minutes, turning occasionally, until the chicken is fully cooked and has a nice char.

In a small bowl, mix together toasted sesame seeds, honey, and soy sauce to create the sesame glaze.

Brush the sesame glaze over the grilled chicken skewers during the last few minutes of cooking.

Once cooked, remove the chicken skewers from the grill.

Garnish with chopped green onions and additional toasted sesame seeds.

Serve these Sesame Teriyaki Chicken Skewers hot, either as an appetizer or as part of a main course.

These Japanese-inspired Sesame Teriyaki Chicken Skewers offer a perfect balance of sweet and savory flavors with a delightful sesame glaze, making them a delicious addition to any meal or gathering.

Japanese Sweet Potato Korokke (Croquettes)

Ingredients:

For the Sweet Potato Mash:

- 2 large Japanese sweet potatoes, peeled and cubed
- 2 tablespoons unsalted butter
- Salt and pepper to taste

For the Korokke Filling:

- Sweet potato mash (prepared as above)
- 1/2 cup cooked ground chicken or beef (optional)
- 1/4 cup finely chopped onion
- 1/4 cup frozen peas, thawed
- 1 tablespoon soy sauce
- 1 teaspoon grated fresh ginger
- 1 teaspoon sesame oil

For Breading and Frying:

- All-purpose flour
- Eggs, beaten
- Panko breadcrumbs

For Serving:

- Tonkatsu sauce or your favorite dipping sauce

Instructions:

Boil or steam the cubed sweet potatoes until tender. Mash them with butter, salt, and pepper until smooth. Set aside.
In a skillet, sauté finely chopped onion until translucent. Add ground chicken or beef (if using) and cook until browned.
Add thawed peas, soy sauce, grated ginger, and sesame oil to the skillet. Stir to combine.
Combine the sautéed mixture with the sweet potato mash, creating the korokke filling. Allow it to cool.

Take a portion of the sweet potato mixture and shape it into a flat, oval patty.
Dredge each patty in flour, dip in beaten eggs, and coat with Panko breadcrumbs.
Heat oil in a pan for frying. Fry the korokke patties until golden brown on both sides.
Drain excess oil on a paper towel.
Serve the Sweet Potato Korokke hot with tonkatsu sauce or your favorite dipping sauce.

These Japanese Sweet Potato Korokke are a delightful twist on traditional croquettes, featuring a sweet potato and savory filling that's crispy on the outside and soft on the inside. Perfect as a side dish or snack!

Japanese-Inspired Nasu Dengaku (Miso-Glazed Eggplant)

Ingredients:

For the Miso Glaze:

- 3 tablespoons white miso paste
- 2 tablespoons mirin
- 1 tablespoon sake (optional)
- 1 tablespoon sugar
- 1 tablespoon soy sauce

For the Eggplant:

- 2 Japanese eggplants, halved lengthwise
- Vegetable oil for brushing
- Sesame seeds for garnish
- Chopped green onions for garnish

Instructions:

Preheat the oven broiler.
In a bowl, whisk together white miso paste, mirin, sake (if using), sugar, and soy sauce to create the miso glaze. Set aside.
Cut the Japanese eggplants in half lengthwise.
Brush the cut sides of the eggplants with vegetable oil.
Place the eggplants on a baking sheet, cut side up.
Broil the eggplants under the preheated broiler for about 5 minutes or until they start to soften and char slightly.
Remove the eggplants from the oven and brush the miso glaze generously over the cut sides.
Return the eggplants to the broiler and broil for an additional 5-7 minutes or until the miso glaze is caramelized and the eggplants are tender.
Sprinkle sesame seeds and chopped green onions over the glazed eggplants.
Serve the Nasu Dengaku hot as a side dish or appetizer.

This Nasu Dengaku recipe showcases the rich flavors of miso-glazed Japanese eggplants, creating a savory and satisfying dish that makes a delightful addition to your Japanese-inspired menu.

Japanese-Inspired Sakura Mochi

Ingredients:

For the Sweet Rice Cake (Domyoji-ko):

- 1 cup sweet rice flour (mochiko)
- 1 cup water
- Cherry blossom essence or pink food coloring (optional)

For the Sweet Red Bean Filling:

- 1 cup sweet red bean paste (anko)

For Wrapping:

- Salt-pickled cherry leaves (sakura leaves) or substitute with salted cherry blossoms (optional)
- Cornstarch for dusting

Instructions:

Prepare the Sweet Rice Cake:
- In a bowl, mix sweet rice flour with water until smooth.
- Add cherry blossom essence or pink food coloring for a pink hue (optional).
- Cook the mixture over low heat, stirring constantly until it thickens into a smooth, sticky dough. Allow it to cool.

Shape the Sweet Rice Cake:
- Dust your hands with cornstarch. Take a small portion of the sweet rice dough and flatten it in your palm.
- Place a small amount of sweet red bean paste in the center and wrap the dough around the filling, shaping it into a round or oval mochi.

Wrap with Cherry Leaves (Optional):
- If using sakura leaves or salted cherry blossoms, wrap each mochi in a leaf with the salted side facing the mochi. Trim excess leaves.

Serve:
- Serve the Sakura Mochi on a plate, with the cherry leaves or blossoms facing up.

Note: Sakura Mochi is often enjoyed during cherry blossom season in Japan. If cherry leaves or blossoms are not available, you can still enjoy the mochi without wrapping.

This Japanese-inspired Sakura Mochi features a sweet rice cake filled with red bean paste, creating a delightful and traditional treat often enjoyed during cherry blossom season.

Japanese Hōtō Nabe (Flat Udon Noodle Hot Pot)

Ingredients:

For the Hōtō Noodles:

- 8 oz (about 225g) flat udon noodles
- 1 tablespoon vegetable oil

For the Broth:

- 6 cups dashi stock
- 1/4 cup soy sauce
- 2 tablespoons mirin
- 1 tablespoon sake (optional)
- 1 tablespoon sugar
- 1 tablespoon miso paste
- 1 carrot, sliced
- 1 leek, sliced
- 1/2 napa cabbage, chopped
- 1 block firm tofu, cubed
- 1 cup shiitake mushrooms, sliced
- Green onions for garnish

Instructions:

In a large pot, heat vegetable oil and sauté the sliced carrot and leek until slightly softened.
Add dashi stock, soy sauce, mirin, sake (if using), sugar, and miso paste to the pot. Bring to a simmer.
Add the flat udon noodles to the pot and cook according to package instructions.
Stir in chopped napa cabbage, tofu cubes, and sliced shiitake mushrooms.
Simmer the Hōtō Nabe until all the ingredients are cooked through and the flavors meld together.
Ladle the hot pot into individual bowls, ensuring each serving has a mix of noodles, vegetables, and tofu.
Garnish with sliced green onions.
Serve the Japanese Hōtō Nabe hot, enjoying the comforting and savory flavors of this flat udon noodle hot pot.

This Hōtō Nabe is a traditional Japanese hot pot dish featuring flat udon noodles, vegetables, and tofu simmered in a flavorful broth. It's a hearty and warming dish perfect for colder days.

Japanese-Inspired Tamago Sando (Egg Sandwich)

Ingredients:

For the Tamagoyaki (Japanese Rolled Omelette):

- 4 large eggs
- 2 tablespoons sugar
- 2 tablespoons mirin
- 1 tablespoon soy sauce
- Vegetable oil for cooking

For the Sandwich:

- Japanese milk bread slices (or your preferred bread)
- Japanese Kewpie mayonnaise
- Fresh chives, finely chopped (optional)

Instructions:

Prepare the Tamagoyaki (Japanese Rolled Omelette):
- In a bowl, whisk together eggs, sugar, mirin, and soy sauce until well combined.
- Heat a rectangular tamagoyaki pan or a small non-stick skillet over medium heat. Brush with a thin layer of vegetable oil.
- Pour a small amount of the egg mixture into the pan, tilting to spread it evenly. Once partially set, roll it towards the far end of the pan.
- Add more egg mixture, lifting the rolled omelette to allow the new mixture to flow underneath. Roll again.
- Repeat the process until all the egg mixture is used. Allow the tamagoyaki to cool and set. Slice into thin rectangles.

Assemble the Tamago Sando:
- Toast the slices of Japanese milk bread if desired.
- Spread a layer of Japanese Kewpie mayonnaise on each slice of bread.
- Arrange slices of tamagoyaki on one slice of bread.
- Top with the second slice of bread to create a sandwich.

Optional:
- Trim the crusts from the sandwich and cut it into bite-sized pieces.

- Sprinkle finely chopped fresh chives over the top for added flavor and garnish.

Serve the Tamago Sando as a delicious and iconic Japanese-style egg sandwich.

This Tamago Sando offers a delightful combination of sweet and savory flavors with the unique texture of Japanese milk bread, making it a popular and tasty choice for breakfast or as a snack.

Japanese-Inspired Gyoza Dumplings

Ingredients:

For the Gyoza Filling:

- 1/2 lb (about 225g) ground pork
- 1 cup cabbage, finely chopped
- 2 cloves garlic, minced
- 1 tablespoon ginger, grated
- 2 green onions, finely chopped
- 1 tablespoon soy sauce
- 1 tablespoon sesame oil
- 1 teaspoon sugar
- 1/2 teaspoon salt
- 1/4 teaspoon black pepper

For the Gyoza Wrappers:

- Store-bought gyoza wrappers

For Dipping Sauce:

- 3 tablespoons soy sauce
- 1 tablespoon rice vinegar
- 1 teaspoon sesame oil
- Red pepper flakes (optional)

Instructions:

In a bowl, combine ground pork, finely chopped cabbage, minced garlic, grated ginger, chopped green onions, soy sauce, sesame oil, sugar, salt, and black pepper. Mix well to create the gyoza filling.

Place a small spoonful of the filling in the center of a gyoza wrapper.

Moisten the edges of the wrapper with water and fold it in half, creating a half-moon shape. Pleat the edges, pressing to seal.

Repeat the process for the remaining wrappers and filling.

Heat a skillet with a bit of oil over medium-high heat. Place the gyoza in the skillet, flat side down, and cook until the bottoms are golden brown.

Carefully add water to the skillet, cover, and steam the gyoza for a few minutes until the filling is cooked through.

In a small bowl, mix together soy sauce, rice vinegar, sesame oil, and red pepper flakes (if using) to create the dipping sauce.

Serve the Japanese-Inspired Gyoza Dumplings hot, with the dipping sauce on the side.

These homemade Gyoza Dumplings offer a delicious combination of juicy pork filling and crispy bottoms, providing a delightful Japanese-inspired appetizer or meal option.

Japanese-Inspired Katsudon (Pork Cutlet Rice Bowl)

Ingredients:

For the Tonkatsu (Pork Cutlet):

- 4 boneless pork loin chops
- Salt and black pepper to taste
- All-purpose flour for dredging
- 2 eggs, beaten
- Panko breadcrumbs for coating
- Vegetable oil for frying

For the Sauce:

- 1 onion, thinly sliced
- 2 tablespoons soy sauce
- 2 tablespoons mirin
- 1 tablespoon sake (optional)
- 1 tablespoon sugar
- 1 cup dashi stock (or substitute with chicken or vegetable broth)

For Assembly:

- Cooked Japanese rice
- Green onions, sliced for garnish
- Pickled red ginger (beni shoga) for garnish
- Nori strips for garnish

Instructions:

Season the pork loin chops with salt and black pepper.
Dredge each pork chop in flour, dip in beaten eggs, and coat with Panko breadcrumbs.
Heat vegetable oil in a pan over medium heat. Fry the pork chops until golden brown and cooked through. Drain on a paper towel.
In a separate pan, sauté thinly sliced onion until softened.
Add soy sauce, mirin, sake (if using), sugar, and dashi stock to the pan. Bring to a simmer.

Cut the fried pork chops into strips and add them to the simmering sauce. Allow the pork to absorb the flavors.
In serving bowls, place a serving of cooked Japanese rice.
Arrange the tonkatsu strips and sauce over the rice.
Garnish with sliced green onions, pickled red ginger, and nori strips.
Serve the Japanese-Inspired Katsudon hot, providing a comforting and flavorful pork cutlet rice bowl.

This Katsudon recipe features crispy pork cutlets in a savory and slightly sweet sauce, served over a bed of steamed rice for a classic and satisfying Japanese dish.

Japanese-Inspired Teriyaki Salmon Bowl

Ingredients:

For the Teriyaki Salmon:

- 4 salmon fillets
- 1/4 cup soy sauce
- 2 tablespoons mirin
- 1 tablespoon sake (optional)
- 1 tablespoon honey
- 1 tablespoon sesame oil
- 2 cloves garlic, minced
- 1 teaspoon grated fresh ginger

For the Bowl:

- Cooked Japanese short-grain rice
- Steamed broccoli florets
- Sliced carrots
- Sliced cucumber
- Avocado slices
- Sesame seeds for garnish
- Chopped green onions for garnish

Instructions:

In a bowl, mix together soy sauce, mirin, sake (if using), honey, sesame oil, minced garlic, and grated ginger to create the teriyaki marinade.
Place the salmon fillets in the marinade, ensuring they are well-coated. Allow the salmon to marinate for at least 30 minutes.
Preheat the oven to 400°F (200°C).
Place the marinated salmon fillets on a baking sheet lined with parchment paper.
Bake the salmon in the preheated oven for 12-15 minutes or until the salmon is cooked through and flakes easily with a fork.
While the salmon is baking, prepare the bowl components. Arrange cooked Japanese short-grain rice in serving bowls and top with steamed broccoli florets, sliced carrots, cucumber slices, and avocado slices.
Once the salmon is done, place a fillet on top of each rice bowl.

Drizzle any remaining teriyaki marinade over the salmon and bowl components.
Garnish the bowl with sesame seeds and chopped green onions.
Serve the Japanese-Inspired Teriyaki Salmon Bowl hot.

This Teriyaki Salmon Bowl offers a delicious combination of tender teriyaki-glazed salmon and fresh vegetables over a bed of fluffy rice, providing a wholesome and flavorful Japanese-inspired meal.

Japanese-Inspired Shrimp Tempura Udon

Ingredients:

For the Tempura Batter:

- 1 cup all-purpose flour
- 1 cup ice-cold water
- 1 egg yolk
- Ice cubes

For the Shrimp Tempura:

- 8 large shrimp, peeled and deveined
- Tempura batter (recipe above)
- Vegetable oil for deep-frying

For the Udon Soup:

- 4 packs of fresh or frozen udon noodles
- 6 cups dashi stock
- 1/4 cup soy sauce
- 2 tablespoons mirin
- 1 tablespoon sake (optional)
- 1 tablespoon sugar
- 1 cup sliced shiitake mushrooms
- 1 cup sliced bok choy
- Green onions, sliced for garnish

Instructions:

Prepare the Tempura Batter:
- In a bowl, combine all-purpose flour, ice-cold water, and egg yolk. Stir until just combined; the batter should be slightly lumpy.
- Add a few ice cubes to keep the batter cold.

Prepare the Shrimp Tempura:
- Heat vegetable oil in a deep fryer or large pot to 350°F (180°C).
- Dip each shrimp in the tempura batter, allowing excess batter to drip off.
- Carefully place the battered shrimp in the hot oil and fry until golden brown and crispy. Remove and drain on paper towels.

Prepare the Udon Soup:
- Cook udon noodles according to package instructions. Drain and set aside.
- In a pot, combine dashi stock, soy sauce, mirin, sake (if using), and sugar. Bring to a simmer.
- Add sliced shiitake mushrooms and bok choy to the simmering broth. Cook until vegetables are tender.

Assemble the Shrimp Tempura Udon:
- Divide the cooked udon noodles among serving bowls.
- Pour the hot udon soup over the noodles, ensuring each bowl has a mix of broth and vegetables.
- Top with crispy shrimp tempura.

Garnish with sliced green onions.

Serve the Japanese-Inspired Shrimp Tempura Udon hot, enjoying the delightful combination of crispy tempura and comforting udon soup.

This Shrimp Tempura Udon combines the crispy goodness of tempura shrimp with the comforting warmth of udon soup, creating a satisfying and flavorful Japanese-inspired dish.

Japanese-Inspired Matcha Latte

Ingredients:

- 1 teaspoon matcha powder
- 1 tablespoon hot water
- 1 cup milk (your choice, such as whole milk, almond milk, or oat milk)
- 1-2 tablespoons honey or sweetener of choice (adjust to taste)

Instructions:

Sift the matcha powder into a bowl to ensure there are no lumps.
Add hot water to the matcha powder and whisk vigorously with a bamboo whisk or a small whisk until a smooth and frothy paste forms.
Heat the milk in a saucepan or using a milk frother until it reaches your desired temperature.
Pour the frothy matcha paste into a cup.
Pour the hot milk over the matcha paste, stirring gently to combine.
Sweeten the matcha latte with honey or your preferred sweetener, adjusting to taste.
Optional: Use a bamboo whisk to create more froth on top of the latte.
Serve the Japanese-Inspired Matcha Latte hot, enjoying the rich and earthy flavors of matcha combined with creamy milk.

This Matcha Latte is a comforting and energizing beverage that highlights the unique and vibrant taste of matcha, making it a popular choice in Japanese tea culture.

Japanese-Inspired Okonomiyaki (Cabbage Pancake)

Ingredients:

For the Okonomiyaki Batter:

- 2 cups shredded cabbage
- 1 cup all-purpose flour
- 1 cup dashi stock
- 2 eggs
- 1/2 cup chopped green onions
- 1/4 cup grated yamaimo (Japanese mountain yam) or substitute with grated regular yam
- Salt and pepper to taste

For Toppings and Filling:

- Thinly sliced pork belly or bacon
- Tenkasu (tempura crumbs) or crushed tempura flakes
- Okonomiyaki sauce (or a mixture of Worcestershire sauce and ketchup)
- Japanese mayonnaise
- Aonori (dried green seaweed flakes)
- Katsuobushi (bonito flakes)

Instructions:

In a large bowl, combine shredded cabbage, all-purpose flour, dashi stock, eggs, chopped green onions, grated yamaimo, salt, and pepper. Mix until well combined to create the okonomiyaki batter.
Heat a griddle or non-stick pan over medium heat. Lightly grease the surface with oil.
Pour a portion of the batter onto the griddle, forming a round pancake. Place a few slices of thinly sliced pork belly or bacon on top.
Cook until the bottom is golden brown, then flip and cook the other side until cooked through and crispy.
Once both sides are cooked, transfer the okonomiyaki to a serving plate.
Drizzle okonomiyaki sauce over the pancake and add dollops of Japanese mayonnaise.
Sprinkle tenkasu or crushed tempura flakes, aonori, and katsuobushi over the top.

Repeat the process for the remaining batter.
Serve the Japanese-Inspired Okonomiyaki hot, slicing it into wedges for easy sharing.

This Okonomiyaki recipe showcases a savory cabbage pancake topped with delicious ingredients, creating a customizable and flavorful dish that is a popular street food in Japan.

Japanese-Inspired Yaki Udon (Stir-Fried Udon Noodles)

Ingredients:

For the Yaki Udon Noodles:

- 8 oz (about 225g) udon noodles
- 2 tablespoons vegetable oil
- 1 onion, thinly sliced
- 1 carrot, julienned
- 1 bell pepper, thinly sliced
- 1 cup shredded cabbage
- 1 cup sliced shiitake mushrooms
- 1 cup sliced cooked chicken, beef, or tofu (optional)
- 3 tablespoons soy sauce
- 2 tablespoons oyster sauce
- 1 tablespoon mirin
- 1 teaspoon sugar
- 1 teaspoon sesame oil

Instructions:

Cook the udon noodles according to package instructions. Drain and set aside.
In a large wok or skillet, heat vegetable oil over medium-high heat.
Add thinly sliced onion, julienned carrot, and sliced bell pepper to the wok. Stir-fry for a few minutes until the vegetables start to soften.
Add shredded cabbage and sliced shiitake mushrooms to the wok. Continue to stir-fry until the vegetables are tender-crisp.
If using, add sliced cooked chicken, beef, or tofu to the wok and stir-fry until heated through.
Add the cooked udon noodles to the wok, tossing to combine with the vegetables and protein.
In a small bowl, mix together soy sauce, oyster sauce, mirin, sugar, and sesame oil. Pour the sauce over the udon noodles and stir-fry to evenly coat.
Continue to cook for a few more minutes until everything is well combined and heated through.
Serve the Japanese-Inspired Yaki Udon hot, offering a delicious and satisfying stir-fried udon noodle dish.

This Yaki Udon recipe features thick udon noodles stir-fried with a variety of colorful vegetables and your choice of protein, creating a flavorful and hearty Japanese-inspired dish.

Sakura Sizzle Stir-Fry

Introduction:

Transport your taste buds to the enchanting landscapes of Japan with this delightful Sakura Sizzle Stir-Fry. This Japanese-inspired dish captures the essence of traditional flavors with a modern twist, creating a harmonious blend of colors, textures, and aromas. Perfect for both casual meals and special occasions, this recipe celebrates the beauty of Japanese cuisine.

Ingredients:

- 1 lb thinly sliced beef (such as sirloin or ribeye)
- 2 cups snap peas, ends trimmed
- 1 red bell pepper, thinly sliced
- 1 yellow bell pepper, thinly sliced
- 1 large carrot, julienned
- 4 green onions, sliced
- 3 cloves garlic, minced
- 1 tablespoon fresh ginger, grated
- 1/2 cup soy sauce
- 2 tablespoons sake
- 2 tablespoons mirin
- 1 tablespoon sesame oil
- 2 tablespoons vegetable oil
- 1 tablespoon toasted sesame seeds (for garnish)
- Cooked white rice (to serve)

Instructions:

Marinate the Beef:
- In a bowl, combine soy sauce, sake, mirin, minced garlic, and grated ginger.
- Add the thinly sliced beef to the marinade, ensuring each piece is well-coated.
- Allow the beef to marinate for at least 30 minutes, or refrigerate for a more intense flavor.

Prepare the Vegetables:
- Heat vegetable oil in a wok or large skillet over medium-high heat.

- Add snap peas, red and yellow bell peppers, julienned carrots, and sliced green onions.
- Stir-fry the vegetables until they are slightly tender but still vibrant in color.

Cook the Marinated Beef:
- Push the vegetables to one side of the wok, making space for the marinated beef.
- Add the marinated beef to the empty side of the wok and stir-fry until the beef is cooked to your liking.

Combine and Finish:
- Once the beef is cooked, combine it with the stir-fried vegetables in the wok.
- Drizzle sesame oil over the mixture and toss everything together until well combined.

Serve:
- Transfer the Sakura Sizzle Stir-Fry to a serving dish.
- Garnish with toasted sesame seeds for an added crunch and nutty flavor.
- Serve over a bed of steamed white rice.

Enjoy the symphony of flavors and textures in this Sakura Sizzle Stir-Fry, a dish that pays homage to the rich culinary heritage of Japan. Whether you're a seasoned home chef or a beginner in the kitchen, this recipe promises a delightful and satisfying dining experience.

Miso Glazed Salmon with Wasabi Mash

Introduction:

Indulge in the exquisite flavors of Japan with our Miso Glazed Salmon with Wasabi Mash. This recipe brings together the rich umami of miso and the delicate, buttery texture of salmon, complemented by the subtle heat of wasabi-infused mashed potatoes. Elevate your dining experience with this Japanese-inspired dish that combines tradition and innovation.

Ingredients:

For Miso Glazed Salmon:

- 4 salmon fillets
- 1/4 cup white miso paste
- 2 tablespoons sake
- 2 tablespoons mirin
- 2 tablespoons soy sauce
- 1 tablespoon honey
- 1 teaspoon grated fresh ginger
- Sesame seeds (for garnish)

For Wasabi Mash:

- 4 large potatoes, peeled and cubed
- 2 tablespoons unsalted butter
- 1/4 cup milk
- 2 teaspoons wasabi paste (adjust to taste)
- Salt and pepper to taste

Instructions:

Prepare Miso Glazed Salmon:
- Preheat your oven to 400°F (200°C).
- In a bowl, whisk together miso paste, sake, mirin, soy sauce, honey, and grated ginger to create the glaze.
- Place salmon fillets on a baking sheet lined with parchment paper.
- Brush the miso glaze over each salmon fillet, ensuring they are evenly coated.

- Bake in the preheated oven for 12-15 minutes or until the salmon is cooked through.

Make Wasabi Mash:
- Boil the peeled and cubed potatoes until they are fork-tender.
- Drain the potatoes and mash them using a potato masher or a fork.
- Add butter, milk, and wasabi paste to the mashed potatoes. Mix until smooth and creamy.
- Season with salt and pepper to taste. Adjust the amount of wasabi according to your desired level of heat.

Serve:
- Plate the Miso Glazed Salmon on a bed of wasabi mash.
- Sprinkle sesame seeds over the salmon for a delightful crunch and added visual appeal.
- Garnish with fresh herbs, such as chopped chives or cilantro, for a burst of freshness.

Experience the harmony of flavors as the sweet and savory miso glaze enhances the succulent salmon, while the wasabi-infused mash adds a unique and spicy kick. Miso Glazed Salmon with Wasabi Mash is a culinary journey that combines the best of Japanese ingredients to create a memorable dining experience.

Teriyaki Tofu and Vegetable Soba Noodles

Introduction:

Embark on a culinary adventure with our Teriyaki Tofu and Vegetable Soba Noodles—a delightful fusion of Japanese flavors and wholesome ingredients. This vegetarian dish features pan-seared tofu glazed in a luscious teriyaki sauce, paired with vibrant stir-fried vegetables and satisfying soba noodles. Immerse yourself in the tastes and textures of Japan with this hearty and nutritious recipe.

Ingredients:

For Teriyaki Tofu:

- 1 block firm tofu, pressed and cubed
- 1/4 cup soy sauce
- 2 tablespoons mirin
- 2 tablespoons sake
- 1 tablespoon brown sugar
- 1 tablespoon sesame oil
- 2 cloves garlic, minced
- 1 teaspoon grated fresh ginger
- 2 green onions, sliced (for garnish)

For Vegetable Soba Noodles:

- 8 oz soba noodles
- 2 tablespoons vegetable oil
- 1 cup broccoli florets
- 1 bell pepper, thinly sliced
- 1 carrot, julienned
- 1 cup snow peas, trimmed
- 3 tablespoons soy sauce
- 1 tablespoon mirin
- 1 tablespoon sesame seeds (for garnish)

Instructions:

    Prepare Teriyaki Tofu:

- In a bowl, whisk together soy sauce, mirin, sake, brown sugar, sesame oil, minced garlic, and grated ginger to create the teriyaki sauce.
- Heat a pan over medium-high heat and add the cubed tofu.
- Pour the teriyaki sauce over the tofu and cook until the tofu is golden brown and glazed with the sauce.

Cook Soba Noodles:
- Cook soba noodles according to package instructions. Drain and set aside.

Stir-Fry Vegetables:
- In a large wok or skillet, heat vegetable oil over medium-high heat.
- Add broccoli, bell pepper, carrot, and snow peas to the wok. Stir-fry until the vegetables are tender-crisp.

Combine Tofu, Vegetables, and Noodles:
- Add the cooked teriyaki tofu to the wok with stir-fried vegetables.
- Toss in the cooked soba noodles.
- Pour soy sauce and mirin over the mixture and toss until well combined.

Serve:
- Transfer the Teriyaki Tofu and Vegetable Soba Noodles to serving plates.
- Garnish with sliced green onions and sesame seeds for a burst of freshness and crunch.

Dive into a bowl of Teriyaki Tofu and Vegetable Soba Noodles, where the savory teriyaki-glazed tofu meets the vibrant medley of stir-fried vegetables and tender soba noodles. This wholesome Japanese-inspired dish promises a symphony of flavors and textures in every bite.

Matcha Green Tea Cheesecake

Introduction:

Savor the delicate essence of Japan with our Matcha Green Tea Cheesecake—an exquisite dessert that beautifully blends the rich, earthy flavors of matcha with the creamy indulgence of cheesecake. Elevate your dessert experience with this harmonious combination, creating a treat that's not only visually stunning but also a celebration of Japanese culinary artistry.

Ingredients:

For the Crust:

- 1 1/2 cups graham cracker crumbs
- 1/4 cup melted unsalted butter
- 2 tablespoons granulated sugar

For the Cheesecake Filling:

- 3 packages (24 oz) cream cheese, softened
- 1 cup granulated sugar
- 3 large eggs
- 1 cup sour cream
- 1/4 cup all-purpose flour
- 2 tablespoons matcha green tea powder
- 1 teaspoon vanilla extract

For Matcha Glaze:

- 1 cup powdered sugar
- 2 tablespoons matcha green tea powder
- 3-4 tablespoons milk
- 1 teaspoon vanilla extract

Instructions:

    Preheat Oven:
- Preheat your oven to 325°F (163°C). Grease a 9-inch springform pan.

    Prepare Crust:

- In a bowl, combine graham cracker crumbs, melted butter, and granulated sugar.
- Press the mixture into the bottom of the prepared springform pan to form the crust.

Make Cheesecake Filling:
- In a large mixing bowl, beat the softened cream cheese until smooth.
- Add granulated sugar and continue to beat until well combined.
- Beat in the eggs, one at a time.
- Add sour cream, flour, matcha green tea powder, and vanilla extract. Mix until smooth and creamy.

Bake:
- Pour the cheesecake filling over the crust in the springform pan.
- Bake in the preheated oven for 55-60 minutes or until the center is set and the top is lightly golden.

Cool and Refrigerate:
- Allow the cheesecake to cool in the pan on a wire rack.
- Once cooled, refrigerate for at least 4 hours or overnight for best results.

Prepare Matcha Glaze:
- In a bowl, whisk together powdered sugar, matcha green tea powder, milk, and vanilla extract until smooth.
- Adjust the consistency by adding more milk if needed.

Glaze and Serve:
- Remove the chilled cheesecake from the springform pan.
- Drizzle the matcha glaze over the top of the cheesecake.
- Slice and serve chilled.

Delight in the captivating flavors of Matcha Green Tea Cheesecake—a luscious dessert that fuses the creaminess of cheesecake with the distinctive taste of matcha, creating a sweet symphony that's sure to leave a lasting impression.

Okonomiyaki - Japanese Savory Pancake

Introduction:

Experience the savory delight of Okonomiyaki, a Japanese savory pancake that brings together a medley of flavors and textures. This versatile dish allows you to customize ingredients to your liking, making it a perfect canvas for creativity. Gather your favorite toppings and dive into the world of Okonomiyaki, where every bite is a culinary adventure.

Ingredients:

For the Batter:

- 2 cups all-purpose flour
- 1 1/2 cups dashi stock (or substitute with water)
- 3 large eggs
- 1/2 cabbage, thinly sliced
- 4 green onions, thinly sliced
- 1/2 cup tenkasu (tempura scraps)
- 1/4 cup pickled red ginger (beni shoga)
- Salt and pepper to taste

For Toppings (Choose your favorites):

- Thinly sliced pork belly or bacon
- Squid or shrimp, chopped
- Bonito flakes
- Japanese mayonnaise
- Okonomiyaki sauce (or tonkatsu sauce)
- Aonori (dried green seaweed flakes)

Instructions:

   Prepare the Batter:
   - In a large bowl, whisk together all-purpose flour, dashi stock (or water), and eggs until smooth.
   - Add thinly sliced cabbage, green onions, tenkasu, pickled red ginger, salt, and pepper. Mix well to combine.

   Cooking Okonomiyaki:

- Heat a griddle or non-stick pan over medium heat.
- Grease the surface with a little oil.
- Pour a ladleful of the batter onto the griddle to form a round pancake.

Add Toppings:
- If using pork belly or bacon, lay slices on top of the pancake.
- Add additional toppings like chopped squid or shrimp as desired.

Flip and Cook:
- Once the edges of the pancake start to set and become golden brown (about 5-7 minutes), carefully flip it using spatulas.
- Cook the other side until golden brown and the center is cooked through.

Serve:
- Transfer the Okonomiyaki to a serving plate.
- Drizzle with Japanese mayonnaise and Okonomiyaki sauce.
- Sprinkle bonito flakes and aonori over the top.

Enjoy:
- Slice the Okonomiyaki into wedges and enjoy the delicious fusion of flavors and textures.

Explore the endless possibilities of Okonomiyaki by choosing your favorite toppings and creating a pancake that suits your taste buds. This Japanese savory pancake is a delightful dish that brings joy to both cooking and eating.

Gyoza - Japanese Pan-Fried Dumplings

Introduction:

Indulge in the delectable world of Gyoza, Japanese pan-fried dumplings that boast a perfect balance of flavors and textures. These bite-sized parcels are filled with a savory mixture of ground meat, vegetables, and aromatic seasonings, creating a delightful combination that's both crispy and tender. Elevate your dining experience with this classic Japanese dish that's perfect for sharing.

Ingredients:

For the Gyoza Filling:

- 1/2 pound ground pork
- 1 cup napa cabbage, finely chopped
- 2 green onions, finely chopped
- 2 cloves garlic, minced
- 1 tablespoon fresh ginger, grated
- 1 tablespoon soy sauce
- 1 teaspoon sesame oil
- 1/2 teaspoon sugar
- 1/2 teaspoon salt
- 1/4 teaspoon black pepper

For the Gyoza Wrappers:

- Gyoza wrappers (store-bought or homemade)

For Dipping Sauce:

- 3 tablespoons soy sauce
- 1 tablespoon rice vinegar
- 1 teaspoon sesame oil
- 1 teaspoon sugar
- 1/2 teaspoon red pepper flakes (optional)

Instructions:

    Prepare Gyoza Filling:

- In a large bowl, combine ground pork, chopped napa cabbage, green onions, minced garlic, grated ginger, soy sauce, sesame oil, sugar, salt, and black pepper.
- Mix the ingredients thoroughly until well combined.

Assemble Gyoza:
- Place a small spoonful of the filling in the center of a gyoza wrapper.
- Moisten the edges of the wrapper with water and fold it in half, creating a half-moon shape.
- Pleat and press the edges together to seal, ensuring no air pockets are trapped inside.

Pan-Fry Gyoza:
- Heat a non-stick skillet over medium-high heat.
- Add a small amount of oil to coat the bottom of the skillet.
- Place the gyoza in the skillet, flat side down, ensuring they are not touching.
- Cook until the bottoms are golden brown.

Steam Gyoza:
- Pour water into the skillet, covering the gyoza halfway.
- Cover the skillet with a lid and steam the gyoza for 5-7 minutes or until the wrappers become translucent.

Crisp Bottoms:
- Remove the lid and let the remaining water evaporate.
- Allow the gyoza to crisp up on the bottom.

Prepare Dipping Sauce:
- In a small bowl, whisk together soy sauce, rice vinegar, sesame oil, sugar, and red pepper flakes (if using).

Serve:
- Transfer the cooked gyoza to a serving plate.
- Serve hot with the dipping sauce.

Delight in the joy of Gyoza—a perfect blend of savory filling, crispy bottoms, and a tangy dipping sauce. Whether enjoyed as a snack, appetizer, or main course, these Japanese pan-fried dumplings are sure to become a favorite in your culinary repertoire.

Chawanmushi - Japanese Steamed Egg Custard

Introduction:

Experience the sublime harmony of flavors and textures with Chawanmushi, a traditional Japanese steamed egg custard. This delicate and savory dish features a velvety smooth egg custard filled with a medley of ingredients such as chicken, shrimp, and mushrooms. Served in individual cups, Chawanmushi is a culinary masterpiece that embodies the essence of Japanese comfort food.

Ingredients:

For the Steamed Egg Custard:

- 4 large eggs
- 2 cups dashi stock
- 2 tablespoons soy sauce
- 1 tablespoon mirin
- 1/2 teaspoon salt

For the Filling:

- 1/2 cup cooked chicken, shredded
- 1/2 cup shrimp, peeled and deveined
- 1/2 cup shiitake mushrooms, thinly sliced
- 1/4 cup ginkgo nuts (optional)
- 1 green onion, thinly sliced
- 1/2 cup kamaboko (fish cake), thinly sliced

Instructions:

Prepare Dashi Stock:
- In a saucepan, combine dashi stock, soy sauce, mirin, and salt. Bring to a gentle simmer and let it cool.

Whisk Eggs:
- In a bowl, whisk the eggs until well beaten.
- Gradually add the cooled dashi mixture to the eggs, stirring continuously.

Strain the Mixture:
- Strain the egg and dashi mixture through a fine-mesh sieve to achieve a smooth consistency.

Assemble Filling:
- Divide the cooked chicken, shrimp, shiitake mushrooms, ginkgo nuts (if using), green onion, and kamaboko evenly among individual chawanmushi cups or small heatproof bowls.

Pour Egg Mixture:
- Gently pour the strained egg and dashi mixture over the filling in each cup.

Steam:
- Place the chawanmushi cups in a steamer basket or on a rack in a large steamer.
- Steam over medium heat for about 15-20 minutes or until the custard is set. Check by inserting a toothpick—if it comes out clean, the custard is ready.

Serve:
- Carefully remove the chawanmushi cups from the steamer.
- Serve the steamed egg custard cups hot, either directly in the cups or unmolded onto serving plates.

Chawanmushi offers a delightful combination of silky-smooth custard and savory goodness from the various ingredients. Enjoy the comforting and nuanced flavors of this Japanese classic as you savor each spoonful of this elegant dish.

Nikujaga - Japanese Meat and Potato Stew

Introduction:

Warm up your senses with Nikujaga, a hearty and comforting Japanese meat and potato stew. This beloved dish features tender slices of beef simmered with potatoes, carrots, and onions in a flavorful soy and mirin-infused broth. Nikujaga is the perfect embodiment of home-cooked comfort, offering a taste of Japanese culinary warmth.

Ingredients:

- 1 lb thinly sliced beef (such as thinly sliced sirloin or ribeye)
- 4 medium potatoes, peeled and cut into bite-sized chunks
- 2 carrots, peeled and sliced into rounds
- 1 large onion, thinly sliced
- 1 cup green beans, ends trimmed and halved (optional)
- 4 cups dashi stock
- 1/3 cup soy sauce
- 1/4 cup mirin
- 2 tablespoons sugar
- 1 tablespoon vegetable oil
- Salt and pepper to taste
- Chopped green onions (for garnish)

Instructions:

Prepare Vegetables:
- Peel and cut the potatoes into bite-sized chunks.
- Peel and slice the carrots into rounds.
- Thinly slice the onion.
- Trim and halve the green beans if using.

Cooking the Stew:
- In a large pot or Dutch oven, heat vegetable oil over medium heat.
- Add thinly sliced beef and cook until browned.

Add Vegetables:
- Add sliced onions to the pot and sauté until softened.
- Stir in potatoes, carrots, and green beans (if using).

Make Broth:
- Pour dashi stock, soy sauce, mirin, and sugar into the pot.

- Bring the mixture to a boil, then reduce the heat to simmer.

Simmer:
- Cover the pot and let the stew simmer for about 20-25 minutes or until the vegetables are tender.

Adjust Seasoning:
- Taste the stew and adjust the seasoning with salt and pepper if needed.

Serve:
- Ladle the Nikujaga into serving bowls.
- Garnish with chopped green onions.

Enjoy:
- Serve the Nikujaga over a bowl of steamed rice and savor the comforting flavors of this classic Japanese meat and potato stew.

Nikujaga is a soul-soothing dish that brings together the heartiness of meat, the wholesomeness of potatoes, and the umami-rich broth. Enjoy the warmth and comforting embrace of this Japanese favorite.

Katsudon - Japanese Pork Cutlet Bowl

Introduction:

Indulge in the satisfying crunch of Katsudon, a beloved Japanese dish featuring crispy pork cutlets nestled on a bed of steamed rice and topped with a savory sweet onion and egg mixture. This flavorful combination creates a comforting and wholesome meal that's as delicious as it is visually appealing.

Ingredients:

For Pork Cutlets (Tonkatsu):

- 4 boneless pork loin chops
- Salt and pepper to taste
- 1 cup all-purpose flour
- 2 large eggs, beaten
- 2 cups panko breadcrumbs
- Vegetable oil for frying

For Onion and Egg Mixture:

- 2 large onions, thinly sliced
- 2 cups dashi stock
- 1/4 cup soy sauce
- 2 tablespoons mirin
- 2 tablespoons sugar
- 4 large eggs, lightly beaten

For Serving:

- Steamed white rice
- Chopped green onions (for garnish)
- Pickled ginger (optional)

Instructions:

    Prepare Pork Cutlets (Tonkatsu):
- Season the pork loin chops with salt and pepper.

- Dredge each pork chop in flour, dip into beaten eggs, and coat with panko breadcrumbs, pressing gently to adhere.

Fry Pork Cutlets:
- In a large skillet, heat vegetable oil over medium-high heat.
- Fry the pork cutlets until golden brown and cooked through, about 4-5 minutes per side. Drain on paper towels.

Make Onion and Egg Mixture:
- In a separate pan, sauté thinly sliced onions until softened.
- Add dashi stock, soy sauce, mirin, and sugar to the onions. Bring to a simmer.

Simmer and Add Eggs:
- Cut the fried pork cutlets into strips and add them to the simmering onion mixture.
- Pour lightly beaten eggs over the pork and onions. Cover and simmer until the eggs are just set.

Serve:
- Spoon the pork, onion, and egg mixture over steamed white rice in serving bowls.
- Garnish with chopped green onions and, if desired, pickled ginger.

Enjoy:
- Dive into the delightful combination of crispy tonkatsu, savory onion and egg mixture, and fluffy rice in each bite of Katsudon.

Katsudon offers a comforting blend of textures and flavors, making it a classic and satisfying Japanese dish that's perfect for a hearty meal. Enjoy the rich taste of the crispy pork cutlets combined with the sweet and savory goodness of the onion and egg mixture.

Yaki Udon - Japanese Stir-Fried Udon Noodles

Introduction:

Satisfy your cravings with Yaki Udon, a delightful Japanese stir-fried noodle dish that combines thick, chewy udon noodles with a flavorful medley of vegetables, protein, and a savory soy-based sauce. Quick to prepare and bursting with umami goodness, Yaki Udon is a versatile and comforting dish that will transport your taste buds to the streets of Japan.

Ingredients:

For Yaki Udon Sauce:

- 3 tablespoons soy sauce
- 2 tablespoons oyster sauce
- 1 tablespoon mirin
- 1 tablespoon sake
- 1 tablespoon sugar
- 1 teaspoon sesame oil

For Stir-Fry:

- 8 oz udon noodles, cooked according to package instructions
- 2 tablespoons vegetable oil
- 2 boneless, skinless chicken thighs, thinly sliced (or protein of your choice)
- 1 cup broccoli florets
- 1 medium carrot, julienned
- 1 bell pepper, thinly sliced
- 1 cup cabbage, thinly sliced
- 3 green onions, sliced
- 2 cloves garlic, minced
- 1 tablespoon grated fresh ginger
- Sesame seeds for garnish

Instructions:

> Prepare Yaki Udon Sauce:
> - In a small bowl, whisk together soy sauce, oyster sauce, mirin, sake, sugar, and sesame oil. Set aside.

Cook Udon Noodles:
- Cook udon noodles according to package instructions. Drain and set aside.

Stir-Fry Chicken and Vegetables:
- Heat vegetable oil in a large wok or skillet over medium-high heat.
- Add sliced chicken thighs and stir-fry until browned and cooked through.
- Add minced garlic and grated ginger, sautéing briefly until fragrant.
- Add broccoli, julienned carrot, bell pepper, and cabbage. Stir-fry until the vegetables are slightly tender but still crisp.

Combine Noodles and Sauce:
- Add the cooked udon noodles to the wok.
- Pour the yaki udon sauce over the noodles and vegetables.
- Toss everything together to ensure the noodles are well-coated with the sauce.

Finish and Garnish:
- Stir in sliced green onions and cook for an additional minute.
- Garnish with sesame seeds for added texture and flavor.

Serve:
- Transfer the Yaki Udon to serving plates.
- Serve hot and enjoy the wonderful combination of flavors and textures.

Yaki Udon is a versatile dish that can be customized with your favorite vegetables and protein. Whether you choose chicken, beef, shrimp, or tofu, the result is a satisfying and delicious stir-fried noodle dish that captures the essence of Japanese street food.

Sunomono - Japanese Cucumber Salad

Introduction:

Refresh your palate with Sunomono, a light and tangy Japanese cucumber salad that's perfect as a side dish or a refreshing appetizer. This simple yet flavorful salad features crisp cucumber slices tossed in a sweet and tangy rice vinegar dressing, creating a delightful balance of flavors that complements a variety of Japanese dishes.

Ingredients:

For the Salad:

- 2 large cucumbers, thinly sliced
- 1/2 red onion, thinly sliced
- 1/4 cup wakame seaweed, rehydrated (optional)
- Sesame seeds for garnish

For the Dressing:

- 1/4 cup rice vinegar
- 2 tablespoons soy sauce
- 1 tablespoon mirin
- 1 tablespoon sugar
- 1 teaspoon sesame oil

Instructions:

> Prepare Cucumbers:
> - Wash the cucumbers and thinly slice them. You can use a mandoline or a knife for uniform slices.
> - If using wakame seaweed, rehydrate it according to the package instructions and set aside.
>
> Make Dressing:
> - In a small bowl, whisk together rice vinegar, soy sauce, mirin, sugar, and sesame oil until the sugar is dissolved.
>
> Assemble Salad:

- In a large bowl, combine the thinly sliced cucumbers, red onion, and rehydrated wakame seaweed (if using).

Toss with Dressing:
- Pour the dressing over the cucumber mixture.
- Toss the salad gently to ensure the cucumber slices are evenly coated with the dressing.

Chill:
- Cover the bowl and refrigerate the Sunomono for at least 30 minutes to allow the flavors to meld.

Serve:
- Before serving, toss the salad once more and transfer it to a serving dish.
- Garnish with sesame seeds for added texture and visual appeal.

Enjoy:
- Serve Sunomono as a refreshing side dish alongside your favorite Japanese meals or enjoy it on its own as a light and cooling appetizer.

Sunomono is a crisp and invigorating salad that brings a burst of flavor to your table. The combination of sweet, tangy, and savory notes makes it a perfect accompaniment to a variety of Japanese dishes, providing a refreshing contrast to richer flavors.

Tamago Sushi - Japanese Sweet Rolled Omelette Sushi

Introduction:

Embark on a culinary journey with Tamago Sushi, a delightful and visually appealing Japanese sushi roll featuring a sweet and fluffy rolled omelette. This sushi variation, known for its unique combination of flavors and textures, is perfect for sushi enthusiasts who appreciate the sweet simplicity of tamago (Japanese omelette) in a sushi form.

Ingredients:

For Tamago (Omelette):

- 4 large eggs
- 2 tablespoons sugar
- 1 tablespoon mirin
- 1 tablespoon soy sauce
- Vegetable oil for cooking

For Sushi Rice:

- 2 cups sushi rice, cooked and seasoned with rice vinegar, sugar, and salt

For Sushi Rolling:

- Nori (seaweed) sheets
- Bamboo sushi rolling mat
- Soy sauce for dipping
- Pickled ginger and wasabi (optional, for serving)

Instructions:

    Prepare Tamago (Omelette):
- In a bowl, whisk together eggs, sugar, mirin, and soy sauce until well combined.
- Heat a non-stick pan over medium heat and lightly coat it with vegetable oil.
- Pour a thin layer of the egg mixture into the pan and swirl to coat the bottom.

- Once the edges start to set, roll the omelette from one end to the other. Push the rolled omelette to the other side of the pan.
- Add another thin layer of the egg mixture to the empty side of the pan, lifting the rolled omelette to let the new layer flow underneath.
- Repeat the rolling process until all the egg mixture is used. Once cooked, set aside to cool.

Prepare Sushi Rice:
- Cook sushi rice according to package instructions.
- Season the cooked rice with a mixture of rice vinegar, sugar, and salt while it is still warm. Allow the rice to cool to room temperature.

Assemble Tamago Sushi:
- Place a sheet of nori on the bamboo sushi rolling mat.
- Wet your hands and spread a thin layer of sushi rice over the nori, leaving a border at the top.
- Place a strip of the rolled tamago omelette along the bottom edge of the rice.

Roll Sushi:
- Carefully lift the bamboo mat and roll the nori and rice over the tamago, using the mat to shape it into a tight cylinder.
- Seal the edge with a bit of water to secure the roll.

Slice and Serve:
- Using a sharp knife, slice the rolled Tamago Sushi into bite-sized pieces.
- Arrange the slices on a serving plate.

Serve with Accompaniments:
- Serve Tamago Sushi with soy sauce for dipping.
- Optionally, include pickled ginger and wasabi on the side for additional flavors.

Tamago Sushi is a delightful addition to your sushi repertoire, combining the sweetness of the rolled omelette with the savory notes of sushi rice and nori. Enjoy the simplicity and elegance of this Japanese sushi variation.

Hōtō Nabe - Japanese Pumpkin and Noodle Hot Pot

Introduction:

Embrace the warmth of a comforting Japanese hot pot with Hōtō Nabe, a hearty and nourishing dish that combines thick wheat noodles, kabocha pumpkin, and a variety of vegetables in a savory miso-based broth. This heartwarming hot pot is perfect for cozy gatherings and provides a delightful taste of Japanese home-style cooking.

Ingredients:

For Broth:

- 6 cups dashi stock
- 1/4 cup soy sauce
- 3 tablespoons miso paste (white or red)
- 1 tablespoon mirin
- 1 tablespoon sake
- 1 tablespoon vegetable oil
- 2 cloves garlic, minced
- 1 tablespoon grated ginger

For Hōtō Nabe:

- 1/2 kabocha pumpkin, peeled, seeds removed, and cut into chunks
- 2 carrots, peeled and sliced
- 1 leek, sliced
- 1 medium onion, thinly sliced
- 1 cup shiitake mushrooms, sliced
- 8 oz thick udon noodles
- 1 cup spinach leaves, washed
- Green onions for garnish

Instructions:

Prepare Broth:
- In a large pot, heat vegetable oil over medium heat.
- Add minced garlic and grated ginger, sautéing until fragrant.
- Pour dashi stock, soy sauce, mirin, and sake into the pot. Bring to a simmer.

- In a small bowl, dissolve miso paste in a ladleful of the broth, then add it back to the pot. Stir well to combine.

Add Vegetables and Pumpkin:
- Add kabocha pumpkin chunks, sliced carrots, leek, onion, and shiitake mushrooms to the simmering broth.
- Let the vegetables cook until they start to soften.

Add Udon Noodles:
- Gently place the thick udon noodles into the pot, ensuring they are submerged in the broth.
- Allow the noodles to cook until tender, following package instructions.

Finish with Spinach:
- Just before serving, add washed spinach leaves to the pot and let them wilt in the hot broth.

Serve:
- Ladle the Hōtō Nabe into individual bowls, making sure each serving has a generous mix of vegetables, pumpkin, and noodles.

Garnish and Enjoy:
- Garnish the hot pot with sliced green onions for freshness.
- Serve immediately, enjoying the comforting flavors of this Japanese pumpkin and noodle hot pot.

Hōtō Nabe brings together the wholesome goodness of seasonal vegetables, pumpkin, and udon noodles in a rich miso-based broth. This Japanese hot pot is a celebration of comforting flavors that warm the heart and soul, making it a perfect choice for chilly evenings.

Gyudon - Japanese Beef Bowl

Introduction:

Savor the rich and savory goodness of Gyudon, a classic Japanese dish featuring thinly sliced beef simmered in a flavorful soy-based sauce, served over a bed of steamed rice. Quick to prepare and bursting with umami, Gyudon is a beloved comfort food that captures the essence of Japanese home-cooked meals.

Ingredients:

- 1 lb thinly sliced beef (such as beef sukiyaki or ribeye)
- 1 large onion, thinly sliced
- 2 cups cooked short-grain rice

For Gyudon Sauce:

- 1/2 cup soy sauce
- 1/4 cup mirin
- 2 tablespoons sake
- 1 tablespoon sugar
- 1 cup dashi stock (or substitute with beef or chicken broth)
- 2 tablespoons vegetable oil

For Garnish:

- Sliced green onions
- Pickled ginger (optional)

Instructions:

   Prepare Gyudon Sauce:
   - In a bowl, whisk together soy sauce, mirin, sake, sugar, and dashi stock. Set aside.

   Cook Thinly Sliced Beef:
   - Heat vegetable oil in a large pan or skillet over medium heat.
   - Add thinly sliced beef to the pan and cook until browned.

   Add Sliced Onions:
   - Add thinly sliced onions to the pan with the beef.
   - Sauté the onions until they become translucent and tender.

Simmer in Gyudon Sauce:
- Pour the Gyudon sauce over the beef and onions in the pan.
- Bring the mixture to a simmer and let it cook for a few minutes, allowing the flavors to meld.

Serve Over Rice:
- Place a portion of steamed rice in individual serving bowls.
- Spoon the beef and onion mixture over the rice.

Garnish and Enjoy:
- Garnish Gyudon with sliced green onions and, if desired, pickled ginger for added flavor.
- Serve immediately and enjoy the comforting and savory Gyudon.

Gyudon is a quick and satisfying meal that captures the essence of Japanese comfort food. The tender slices of beef, caramelized onions, and flavorful sauce create a perfect harmony that makes Gyudon a favorite among those who appreciate the simplicity and deliciousness of Japanese cuisine.

Ebi Chili - Japanese Spicy Chili Shrimp

Introduction:

Spice up your dining experience with Ebi Chili, a mouthwatering Japanese dish that features succulent shrimp coated in a flavorful and spicy chili sauce. This vibrant and aromatic dish is perfect as an appetizer or a main course, offering a delightful balance of heat, sweetness, and umami.

Ingredients:

For the Shrimp:

- 1 lb large shrimp, peeled and deveined
- 1/2 cup cornstarch for coating
- Vegetable oil for frying

For the Chili Sauce:

- 2 tablespoons vegetable oil
- 3 cloves garlic, minced
- 1 tablespoon grated ginger
- 1/4 cup soy sauce
- 2 tablespoons sweet chili sauce
- 1 tablespoon oyster sauce
- 1 tablespoon rice vinegar
- 1 tablespoon mirin
- 1 tablespoon sugar
- 1 teaspoon chili paste (adjust to taste)
- 2 green onions, sliced (for garnish)

Instructions:

   Prepare Shrimp:
- Pat the peeled and deveined shrimp dry with paper towels.
- Coat each shrimp in cornstarch, shaking off excess.

   Fry Shrimp:
- Heat vegetable oil in a deep pan or wok over medium-high heat.
- Fry the coated shrimp in batches until they turn golden brown and crispy.

- Remove the shrimp and place them on a paper towel-lined plate to drain excess oil.

Make Chili Sauce:
- In a separate pan, heat vegetable oil over medium heat.
- Add minced garlic and grated ginger, sautéing until fragrant.
- Add soy sauce, sweet chili sauce, oyster sauce, rice vinegar, mirin, sugar, and chili paste to the pan. Stir well to combine.
- Allow the sauce to simmer and thicken for a few minutes.

Coat Shrimp in Chili Sauce:
- Add the fried shrimp to the chili sauce, tossing them until well coated.
- Cook for an additional minute to let the flavors meld.

Garnish and Serve:
- Transfer the Ebi Chili to a serving plate.
- Garnish with sliced green onions.

Enjoy:
- Serve the Ebi Chili as a spicy and flavorful appetizer or as a main course over steamed rice.

Ebi Chili showcases the perfect harmony of crispy shrimp and a spicy-sweet chili sauce. This Japanese dish is sure to tantalize your taste buds with its bold flavors and make a memorable addition to your culinary repertoire.

Chirashi Sushi - Japanese Scattered Sushi Bowl

Introduction:

Experience the beauty and flavors of Chirashi Sushi, a vibrant and visually appealing Japanese dish that translates to "scattered sushi." Chirashi Sushi features a colorful assortment of fresh sashimi, vegetables, and pickles arranged over a bed of seasoned sushi rice. This celebratory dish is perfect for special occasions and showcases the essence of Japanese culinary artistry.

Ingredients:

For Sushi Rice:

- 2 cups sushi rice, cooked and seasoned with rice vinegar, sugar, and salt

For Toppings:

- Assorted sashimi (salmon, tuna, shrimp, etc.), thinly sliced
- Avocado, sliced
- Cucumber, julienned
- Radishes, thinly sliced
- Pickled ginger (gari)
- Soy sauce and wasabi for serving

For Garnish:

- Sesame seeds
- Chopped green onions
- Furikake (Japanese rice seasoning)

Instructions:

   Prepare Sushi Rice:
   - Cook sushi rice according to package instructions.
   - Season the cooked rice with a mixture of rice vinegar, sugar, and salt. Allow it to cool to room temperature.

   Arrange Sushi Rice:
   - Spread the seasoned sushi rice evenly in a large serving bowl or individual bowls.

Add Assorted Toppings:
- Arrange thinly sliced sashimi, avocado slices, julienned cucumber, and radish slices over the sushi rice. Be creative with the arrangement for a visually appealing presentation.

Garnish:
- Sprinkle sesame seeds, chopped green onions, and furikake over the toppings for added flavor and texture.

Serve with Accompaniments:
- Serve Chirashi Sushi with pickled ginger (gari), soy sauce, and wasabi on the side.

Enjoy:
- Dive into the delightful medley of flavors and textures as you enjoy the assorted sashimi and fresh vegetables atop the seasoned sushi rice.

Chirashi Sushi is a feast for the eyes and the palate, offering a delightful array of colors, textures, and flavors. This Japanese scattered sushi bowl is a celebration of freshness and artistry, making it a perfect choice for special occasions or when you want to treat yourself to a visually stunning and delicious meal.

Okonomiyaki - Japanese Savory Pancake

Introduction:

Delight in the savory goodness of Okonomiyaki, a popular Japanese street food that combines a flavorful pancake batter with a variety of ingredients, creating a customizable and delicious dish. Known as "Japanese savory pancake" or "Japanese pizza," Okonomiyaki is a versatile treat that can be tailored to suit your taste preferences.

Ingredients:

For Okonomiyaki Batter:

- 2 cups all-purpose flour
- 1 1/2 cups dashi stock
- 2 large eggs
- 1/2 cabbage, thinly shredded
- 2 green onions, thinly sliced
- 1/2 cup tenkasu (tempura scraps) or tempura flakes
- 1/4 cup pickled red ginger (beni shoga), chopped (optional)
- Salt and pepper to taste

For Toppings and Garnish:

- Thinly sliced pork belly or bacon strips
- Okonomiyaki sauce
- Japanese mayonnaise
- Bonito flakes (katsuobushi)
- Aonori (dried green seaweed flakes)
- Chopped green onions

Instructions:

Prepare Okonomiyaki Batter:
- In a large bowl, combine all-purpose flour, dashi stock, and eggs.
- Mix until a smooth batter is formed.
- Add shredded cabbage, sliced green onions, tenkasu or tempura flakes, and pickled red ginger (if using) to the batter.
- Season with salt and pepper. Mix well to combine.

Cook Okonomiyaki:
- Heat a griddle or non-stick skillet over medium heat.
- Pour a ladleful of the batter onto the griddle, spreading it into a round pancake shape.
- Arrange thinly sliced pork belly or bacon strips on top of the batter.

Flip and Cook:
- Once the bottom is golden brown and the edges are set, carefully flip the Okonomiyaki using a spatula.
- Cook the other side until it is golden brown and the center is cooked through.

Serve:
- Transfer the cooked Okonomiyaki to a serving plate.

Top and Garnish:
- Drizzle Okonomiyaki sauce and Japanese mayonnaise over the top in a zigzag pattern.
- Sprinkle bonito flakes, aonori, and chopped green onions for garnish.

Enjoy:
- Serve Okonomiyaki hot and enjoy the savory and flavorful combination of the pancake, toppings, and sauces.

Okonomiyaki is a fun and customizable dish that allows you to get creative with toppings and flavors. Whether you prefer it with meat, seafood, or vegetarian, Okonomiyaki is a delightful treat that captures the essence of Japanese street food culture.

Miso Soup with Tofu and Wakame

Introduction:

Experience the comforting and nourishing flavors of Miso Soup with Tofu and Wakame, a classic Japanese soup that combines rich miso paste, silken tofu, and tender wakame seaweed. This soul-soothing soup is quick to prepare and offers a harmonious blend of umami and warmth, making it a staple in Japanese cuisine.

Ingredients:

- 4 cups dashi stock
- 3 tablespoons miso paste (white or red, according to preference)
- 1/2 cup tofu, cubed
- 2 tablespoons dried wakame seaweed, rehydrated
- 2 green onions, thinly sliced
- 1 tablespoon soy sauce (optional)
- 1 teaspoon sesame oil (optional)

Instructions:

Prepare Dashi Stock:
- In a pot, heat 4 cups of dashi stock. Bring it to a gentle simmer.

Rehydrate Wakame:
- Place the dried wakame seaweed in a bowl of water and let it rehydrate for about 5 minutes. Drain and set aside.

Add Tofu to Dashi:
- Once the dashi is simmering, add cubed tofu to the pot. Allow it to simmer for a few minutes until the tofu is heated through.

Dissolve Miso Paste:
- In a small bowl, dissolve miso paste in a ladleful of the hot dashi. Stir until the miso paste is fully dissolved.

Add Miso to Soup:
- Lower the heat and gently whisk the dissolved miso paste into the simmering dashi and tofu mixture.

Add Wakame:
- Add the rehydrated wakame seaweed to the soup. Simmer for an additional 2-3 minutes.

Adjust Seasoning:

- Taste the soup and adjust the flavor with soy sauce if needed. Be cautious with the saltiness, as miso paste is naturally salty.

Finish with Green Onions and Sesame Oil:
- Just before serving, stir in thinly sliced green onions.
- Optionally, drizzle sesame oil over the top for added aroma and flavor.

Serve Hot:
- Ladle the Miso Soup with Tofu and Wakame into bowls.
- Serve hot and enjoy the comforting and nourishing goodness of this classic Japanese soup.

Miso Soup with Tofu and Wakame is a simple yet satisfying soup that showcases the versatility of miso paste and the delicate flavors of tofu and seaweed. It's a wonderful way to start a Japanese meal or enjoy as a light and comforting dish on its own.

Hiyashi Chuka - Japanese Cold Ramen Salad

Introduction:

Cool down on a warm day with Hiyashi Chuka, a refreshing Japanese cold ramen salad featuring chilled ramen noodles topped with a colorful array of vegetables, thinly sliced ham, and a flavorful sesame dressing. This vibrant dish is both visually appealing and bursting with refreshing flavors, making it a popular choice during the hotter months.

Ingredients:

For Hiyashi Chuka Noodles:

- 8 oz ramen noodles
- Ice water for cooling

For Toppings:

- 1 cucumber, julienned
- 1 carrot, julienned
- 1/2 red bell pepper, thinly sliced
- 1/2 yellow bell pepper, thinly sliced
- 4 slices of ham, thinly sliced
- 2 sheets of nori (seaweed), cut into thin strips
- 2 boiled eggs, halved

For Sesame Dressing:

- 3 tablespoons soy sauce
- 2 tablespoons rice vinegar
- 1 tablespoon sesame oil
- 1 tablespoon sugar
- 1 teaspoon grated ginger
- 1 clove garlic, minced

Instructions:

Cook Ramen Noodles:
- Cook the ramen noodles according to package instructions.

- Drain and immediately rinse the noodles under cold running water to stop the cooking process.

Chill Noodles:
- Transfer the rinsed noodles to a bowl of ice water. Let them cool completely, then drain.

Prepare Sesame Dressing:
- In a small bowl, whisk together soy sauce, rice vinegar, sesame oil, sugar, grated ginger, and minced garlic. Set aside.

Assemble Hiyashi Chuka:
- Place the chilled ramen noodles in serving bowls.
- Arrange julienned cucumber, carrot, sliced red and yellow bell peppers, thinly sliced ham, nori strips, and boiled egg halves on top of the noodles.

Drizzle with Sesame Dressing:
- Drizzle the prepared sesame dressing over the Hiyashi Chuka.

Toss and Serve:
- Gently toss the ingredients to coat them in the dressing.
- Serve immediately, enjoying the refreshing flavors of this cold ramen salad.

Hiyashi Chuka is a delightful dish that combines the freshness of crisp vegetables, the savory notes of ham, and the richness of sesame dressing over chilled ramen noodles. It's a perfect choice for a light and satisfying meal, especially during warm weather.

Yakitori - Japanese Grilled Chicken Skewers

Introduction:

Indulge in the savory delight of Yakitori, a popular Japanese street food featuring skewers of tender grilled chicken brushed with a flavorful soy-based sauce. Whether enjoyed as a snack, appetizer, or part of a meal, Yakitori brings together the smoky aroma of the grill and the umami-rich taste of the sauce for a truly satisfying experience.

Ingredients:

For Chicken Skewers:

- 1 lb boneless, skinless chicken thighs, cut into bite-sized pieces
- Bamboo skewers, soaked in water for 30 minutes

For Yakitori Sauce:

- 1/4 cup soy sauce
- 3 tablespoons sake
- 2 tablespoons mirin
- 2 tablespoons sugar

For Garnish (optional):

- Shichimi togarashi (Japanese seven spice)
- Chopped green onions

Instructions:

Prepare Yakitori Sauce:
- In a small saucepan, combine soy sauce, sake, mirin, and sugar.
- Heat the mixture over medium heat, stirring until the sugar dissolves.
- Simmer for a few minutes until the sauce thickens slightly. Set aside to cool.

Thread Chicken onto Skewers:
- Thread the bite-sized chicken pieces onto the soaked bamboo skewers, leaving a little space between each piece.

Preheat Grill:
- Preheat a grill or grill pan to medium-high heat.

Grill Chicken Skewers:
- Place the chicken skewers on the preheated grill.
- Grill each side for about 3-4 minutes or until the chicken is fully cooked and has a nice char.

Brush with Yakitori Sauce:
- Brush the grilled chicken skewers with the prepared Yakitori sauce, turning them to coat all sides.
- Continue grilling for an additional minute on each side, brushing with more sauce as needed.

Garnish and Serve:
- Transfer the Yakitori skewers to a serving plate.
- Sprinkle with shichimi togarashi and chopped green onions for added flavor and color.

Enjoy:
- Serve the Yakitori skewers hot and enjoy the irresistible combination of smoky grilled chicken and savory Yakitori sauce.

Yakitori is a beloved Japanese street food that captures the essence of grilled perfection and bold flavors. Whether enjoyed as a snack or part of a meal, these grilled chicken skewers are sure to be a hit with friends and family.

Nikujaga - Japanese Meat and Potato Stew

Introduction:

Warm your soul with Nikujaga, a comforting Japanese meat and potato stew that combines tender chunks of beef, potatoes, and vegetables in a sweet and savory soy-based broth. This hearty dish is a staple of Japanese home cooking and offers a satisfying blend of flavors and textures.

Ingredients:

- 1 lb beef (sirloin or chuck), thinly sliced
- 4 medium potatoes, peeled and cut into chunks
- 2 carrots, peeled and sliced
- 1 onion, thinly sliced
- 1 cup green beans, ends trimmed and cut into bite-sized pieces
- 2 cups dashi stock
- 1/4 cup soy sauce
- 3 tablespoons mirin
- 2 tablespoons sugar
- 2 tablespoons vegetable oil

Instructions:

Prepare Ingredients:
- Thinly slice the beef, peel and cut the potatoes into chunks, peel and slice the carrots, thinly slice the onion, and cut the green beans into bite-sized pieces.

Cook Beef:
- Heat vegetable oil in a large pot over medium heat.
- Add thinly sliced beef and cook until browned.

Add Vegetables:
- Add sliced onions to the pot and sauté until they become translucent.
- Add potatoes, carrots, and green beans to the pot.

Prepare Broth:
- Pour dashi stock, soy sauce, mirin, and sugar into the pot.
- Stir to combine the ingredients.

Simmer:
- Bring the stew to a simmer, then reduce the heat to low.

- Cover the pot and let it simmer for about 20-25 minutes or until the potatoes are tender.

Adjust Seasoning:
- Taste the stew and adjust the seasoning if needed, adding more soy sauce, mirin, or sugar according to your preference.

Serve:
- Ladle the Nikujaga into serving bowls.
- Serve hot and enjoy the heartwarming flavors of this traditional Japanese meat and potato stew.

Nikujaga is a beloved Japanese comfort dish that showcases the heartiness of meat and the comforting texture of potatoes. This stew is a classic example of the homey and comforting meals that are deeply ingrained in Japanese culinary traditions.

Katsudon - Japanese Pork Cutlet Bowl

Introduction:

Indulge in the crispy and tender goodness of Katsudon, a classic Japanese dish featuring a deep-fried pork cutlet served over a bowl of rice and topped with a savory sweet soy-based broth and a perfectly cooked egg. This comforting and flavorful dish is a favorite among lovers of Japanese cuisine.

Ingredients:

For Pork Cutlets (Tonkatsu):

- 4 pork loin or pork tenderloin cutlets
- Salt and pepper for seasoning
- All-purpose flour for dredging
- 2 large eggs, beaten
- Panko breadcrumbs for coating
- Vegetable oil for frying

For Katsudon Sauce:

- 2 cups dashi stock
- 1/4 cup soy sauce
- 3 tablespoons mirin
- 2 tablespoons sugar

For Assembly:

- Cooked Japanese rice
- 4 eggs
- Sliced green onions for garnish

Instructions:

    Prepare Pork Cutlets (Tonkatsu):
- Season the pork cutlets with salt and pepper.

- Dredge each cutlet in flour, dip into beaten eggs, and coat with Panko breadcrumbs.
- Heat vegetable oil in a pan over medium heat. Fry the pork cutlets until golden brown and cooked through. Set aside on a paper towel to drain excess oil.

Make Katsudon Sauce:
- In a separate pan, combine dashi stock, soy sauce, mirin, and sugar. Bring the mixture to a simmer and let it cook for a few minutes until the sugar dissolves. Set aside.

Assemble Katsudon:
- Slice the fried pork cutlets into strips.
- Place a serving of cooked Japanese rice in individual bowls.
- Arrange sliced pork cutlets over the rice.

Cook Eggs:
- In a bowl, beat one egg for each serving of Katsudon.
- Pour the beaten egg over the pork cutlets in the pan. Allow it to cook until the edges set.

Pour Sauce and Finish:
- Pour a portion of the Katsudon sauce over the pork and eggs in the pan.
- Continue cooking until the eggs are just set but still slightly runny.

Serve:
- Carefully transfer the pork, egg, and sauce mixture onto the rice in each bowl.
- Garnish with sliced green onions.

Enjoy:
- Serve Katsudon hot, allowing the savory sauce and tender pork cutlet to meld with the rice and egg for a comforting and delicious experience.

Katsudon is a quintessential Japanese dish that combines the satisfaction of crispy fried pork cutlets with the comfort of a rice bowl and flavorful sauce. Enjoy the delightful harmony of textures and flavors in this classic Japanese favorite.

Gomae - Japanese Spinach Salad with Sesame Dressing

Introduction:

Delight in the simplicity and richness of Gomae, a classic Japanese spinach salad featuring blanched spinach dressed in a flavorful sesame sauce. This dish highlights the elegance of minimalism while offering a burst of nutty and savory flavors. Enjoy Gomae as a refreshing side dish or a light appetizer.

Ingredients:

- 1 lb fresh spinach, washed and trimmed
- 2 tablespoons toasted sesame seeds
- 2 tablespoons soy sauce
- 1 tablespoon sugar
- 1 tablespoon mirin
- 1 tablespoon sesame oil

Instructions:

Blanch Spinach:
- Bring a large pot of water to a boil.
- Add the fresh spinach to the boiling water and blanch for about 1-2 minutes until just wilted.
- Immediately transfer the blanched spinach to a bowl of ice water to stop the cooking process.

Drain and Squeeze Spinach:
- Drain the cooled spinach and gently squeeze out excess water.

Prepare Sesame Sauce:
- In a small pan over low heat, toast sesame seeds until golden and fragrant.
- Grind the toasted sesame seeds using a mortar and pestle or a spice grinder until you achieve a coarse texture.
- In a bowl, combine ground sesame seeds, soy sauce, sugar, mirin, and sesame oil. Mix well to create the sesame dressing.

Dress Spinach:
- Place the drained and squeezed spinach on a serving plate.
- Drizzle the sesame dressing over the spinach, ensuring an even coating.

Garnish and Serve:

- Optionally, sprinkle a few additional whole toasted sesame seeds over the top for garnish.

Enjoy:
- Serve Gomae at room temperature or chilled, allowing the flavors of the sesame dressing to infuse the blanched spinach.

Gomae is a delightful and healthy Japanese spinach salad that showcases the natural flavors of fresh spinach enhanced by the nutty richness of sesame. This dish is a perfect addition to any Japanese meal, offering a balance of textures and tastes that elevate the dining experience.

Yaki Udon - Japanese Stir-Fried Udon Noodles

Introduction:

Savor the wok-kissed flavors of Yaki Udon, a popular Japanese stir-fried noodle dish that combines thick udon noodles with a medley of colorful vegetables, protein, and a savory soy-based sauce. Quick and versatile, Yaki Udon is a delicious way to experience the wonderful textures and tastes of Japanese cuisine.

Ingredients:

- 8 oz udon noodles, cooked according to package instructions
- 1 cup thinly sliced chicken, beef, pork, or tofu
- 1 onion, thinly sliced
- 1 bell pepper (any color), thinly sliced
- 1 carrot, julienned
- 1 cup cabbage, thinly sliced
- 2 tablespoons vegetable oil
- 2 cloves garlic, minced
- 1/4 cup soy sauce
- 2 tablespoons oyster sauce
- 1 tablespoon mirin
- 1 tablespoon sake (optional)
- 1 teaspoon sugar
- 1 tablespoon sesame oil
- Green onions, sliced, for garnish

Instructions:

Cook Udon Noodles:
- Cook udon noodles according to package instructions. Drain and set aside.

Prepare Ingredients:
- Thinly slice the choice of protein (chicken, beef, pork, or tofu) and prepare the vegetables (onion, bell pepper, carrot, cabbage).

Stir-Fry Ingredients:
- Heat vegetable oil in a wok or large pan over medium-high heat.
- Add minced garlic and sliced protein. Stir-fry until the protein is cooked through.

Add Vegetables:
- Add sliced onion, bell pepper, julienned carrot, and sliced cabbage to the wok. Stir-fry until the vegetables are tender-crisp.

Prepare Sauce:
- In a small bowl, mix soy sauce, oyster sauce, mirin, sake (if using), sugar, and sesame oil.

Combine Noodles and Sauce:
- Add the cooked udon noodles to the wok.
- Pour the sauce over the noodles and vegetables. Toss everything together to ensure even coating.

Finish and Garnish:
- Continue stir-frying until the udon noodles are heated through and well-coated with the sauce.
- Garnish with sliced green onions.

Serve Hot:
- Transfer Yaki Udon to serving plates.
- Serve hot and enjoy the delicious stir-fried goodness of this Japanese noodle dish.

Yaki Udon is a versatile and flavorful dish that offers a perfect balance of textures and tastes. Whether you choose to include meat, tofu, or a variety of vegetables, this stir-fried udon noodles recipe allows you to customize the dish to your liking.

Chawanmushi - Japanese Steamed Egg Custard

Introduction:

Experience the delicate and silky texture of Chawanmushi, a traditional Japanese steamed egg custard that features a harmonious blend of savory ingredients. This savory custard is not only visually appealing but also a delightful way to showcase the subtle flavors of various ingredients within a silky egg base.

Ingredients:

For Egg Custard Base:

- 4 large eggs
- 2 1/2 cups dashi stock
- 1 tablespoon soy sauce
- 1 tablespoon mirin
- Salt to taste

For Filling (Customizable):

- Cooked chicken slices
- Shrimp, peeled and deveined
- Shiitake mushrooms, sliced
- Ginkgo nuts (optional)
- Kamaboko (fish cake), sliced
- Snow peas, blanched
- Mitsuba (Japanese parsley) for garnish

Instructions:

Prepare Dashi Stock:
- If using instant dashi powder, dissolve it in hot water according to package instructions.
- Alternatively, you can make dashi stock from kombu seaweed and bonito flakes by simmering them in water. Strain the liquid and set aside.

Make Egg Custard Base:
- In a bowl, lightly beat the eggs.

- Gradually add dashi stock while stirring continuously to avoid forming bubbles.
- Add soy sauce, mirin, and a pinch of salt. Mix well.

Strain Custard Mixture:
- Strain the egg custard mixture through a fine mesh sieve to achieve a smooth texture.

Prepare Filling Ingredients:
- Prepare and cook the chosen filling ingredients such as chicken slices, shrimp, shiitake mushrooms, ginkgo nuts, kamaboko, and blanched snow peas.

Assemble Chawanmushi:
- Divide the cooked filling ingredients evenly among individual chawanmushi cups or small heatproof bowls.

Pour Egg Custard Mixture:
- Pour the strained egg custard mixture over the filling ingredients in each cup or bowl.

Steam Chawanmushi:
- Cover the cups or bowls with lids or aluminum foil.
- Steam the Chawanmushi in a steamer for about 15-20 minutes or until the custard is set.

Garnish and Serve:
- Garnish each Chawanmushi cup with mitsuba (Japanese parsley).
- Serve hot as an appetizer or side dish.

Chawanmushi is a delicate and comforting dish that highlights the silky texture of steamed egg custard combined with a variety of flavorful ingredients. Enjoy the subtlety and elegance of this Japanese culinary gem.

Sunomono - Japanese Cucumber Salad

Introduction:

Refresh your palate with Sunomono, a light and tangy Japanese cucumber salad that is both simple and refreshing. This classic dish features thinly sliced cucumbers dressed in a sweet and vinegary sauce, making it an ideal accompaniment to a variety of Japanese meals.

Ingredients:

- 2 Japanese cucumbers or 1 English cucumber, thinly sliced
- 1/4 cup rice vinegar
- 2 tablespoons soy sauce
- 2 tablespoons mirin
- 1 tablespoon sugar
- 1 teaspoon sesame oil
- Toasted sesame seeds for garnish
- Thinly sliced red chili or shichimi togarashi (optional, for heat)
- Chopped fresh cilantro or mint for garnish (optional)

Instructions:

Prepare Cucumbers:
- Wash the cucumbers thoroughly. If using Japanese cucumbers or English cucumber, you can leave the skin on for added texture.
- Thinly slice the cucumbers using a mandoline or a sharp knife. If the cucumber has large seeds, you can remove them with a spoon before slicing.

Make Sunomono Dressing:
- In a bowl, combine rice vinegar, soy sauce, mirin, sugar, and sesame oil. Whisk the ingredients together until the sugar is completely dissolved.

Marinate Cucumbers:
- Place the thinly sliced cucumbers in a shallow dish or bowl.
- Pour the Sunomono dressing over the cucumbers, ensuring they are well coated.
- Toss the cucumbers gently to evenly distribute the dressing.

Chill:

- Cover the dish or bowl with plastic wrap and let the cucumbers marinate in the refrigerator for at least 30 minutes to allow the flavors to meld.

Garnish and Serve:
- Before serving, sprinkle toasted sesame seeds over the cucumbers.
- Optionally, garnish with thinly sliced red chili or shichimi togarashi for a bit of heat.
- For added freshness, you can garnish with chopped fresh cilantro or mint.

Enjoy:
- Serve Sunomono as a refreshing side dish or as part of a Japanese meal.

Sunomono is a palate-cleansing and crisp cucumber salad that perfectly complements the umami-rich flavors of Japanese cuisine. It's a versatile dish that adds a burst of freshness to your dining experience.

Dorayaki - Japanese Red Bean Pancake Sandwiches

Introduction:

Indulge in the delightful sweetness of Dorayaki, a popular Japanese confection that consists of fluffy pancake-like cakes filled with sweet red bean paste. These delightful treats are not only delicious but also capture the essence of traditional Japanese flavors.

Ingredients:

For Dorayaki Pancakes:

- 2 large eggs
- 1/2 cup sugar
- 1 tablespoon honey
- 1 cup all-purpose flour
- 1 teaspoon baking powder
- 1/2 cup water
- Vegetable oil for cooking

For Sweet Red Bean Filling:

- 1 cup sweet red bean paste (anko)

Instructions:

Make Dorayaki Pancake Batter:
- In a bowl, whisk together eggs, sugar, and honey until well combined.
- Sift in the all-purpose flour and baking powder into the egg mixture. Mix well.
- Gradually add water to the batter, whisking continuously until a smooth consistency is achieved.

Cook Dorayaki Pancakes:
- Heat a non-stick skillet or griddle over medium heat.
- Lightly grease the surface with vegetable oil.
- Spoon a portion of the pancake batter onto the skillet to form a small, round pancake. Cook until bubbles form on the surface and the edges appear set.

Flip and Cook:

- Carefully flip the pancake and cook the other side until golden brown.
- Remove the cooked pancake from the skillet and set it aside.

Repeat:
- Repeat the process until all the batter is used, making a stack of pancakes.

Prepare Sweet Red Bean Filling:
- If using canned sweet red bean paste, you can use it as is. If making from scratch, cook and sweeten red beans to form a smooth paste.

Assemble Dorayaki:
- Take one pancake and spread a generous layer of sweet red bean paste on top.
- Place another pancake on top to create a sandwich, pressing gently to adhere.

Serve:
- Repeat the process for the remaining pancakes.
- Serve Dorayaki at room temperature and enjoy the sweet and delightful treat.

Dorayaki is a beloved Japanese dessert that combines the soft and spongy texture of pancakes with the sweet richness of red bean paste. Whether enjoyed with a cup of tea or as a sweet indulgence, Dorayaki is sure to satisfy your cravings for a delightful Japanese treat.

Oyakodon - Japanese Chicken and Egg Rice Bowl

Introduction:

Delight in the comforting flavors of Oyakodon, a classic Japanese dish that translates to "parent and child bowl." This heartwarming dish features tender chicken and beaten eggs cooked in a savory soy-based broth, served over a bed of steamed rice. Oyakodon is not only delicious but also quick and easy to prepare.

Ingredients:

- 2 boneless, skinless chicken thighs, thinly sliced
- 1 onion, thinly sliced
- 3 large eggs, beaten
- 1 cup dashi stock
- 3 tablespoons soy sauce
- 2 tablespoons mirin
- 1 tablespoon sugar
- 2 cups steamed Japanese rice
- Chopped green onions for garnish
- Nori (seaweed) strips for garnish (optional)

Instructions:

Prepare Chicken and Onion:
- Thinly slice the boneless, skinless chicken thighs.
- Thinly slice the onion.

Make Dashi Stock:
- In a pot, combine dashi stock, soy sauce, mirin, and sugar. Bring the mixture to a simmer over medium heat.

Cook Chicken and Onion:
- Add the sliced chicken and onions to the simmering broth.
- Cook until the chicken is cooked through and the onions are tender.

Add Beaten Eggs:
- Once the chicken and onions are cooked, pour the beaten eggs evenly over the mixture.
- Allow the eggs to set slightly, stirring gently to distribute them throughout the broth.

Serve Over Rice:

- Place a portion of steamed Japanese rice in serving bowls.
- Spoon the chicken, onion, and egg mixture over the rice.

Garnish:
- Garnish Oyakodon with chopped green onions and nori strips (if using).

Serve Hot:
- Serve Oyakodon hot and enjoy the comforting combination of tender chicken, savory broth, and fluffy eggs over rice.

Oyakodon is a wholesome and satisfying dish that captures the essence of home-cooked comfort in Japanese cuisine. The name "Oyakodon" reflects the idea of a parent (chicken) and child (egg) coming together in a delicious harmony.

Gyu Don - Japanese Beef Bowl

Introduction:

Savor the rich and savory flavors of Gyu Don, a popular Japanese dish featuring thinly sliced beef simmered in a flavorful soy-based broth, served over a bed of steamed rice. This quick and comforting meal is perfect for those who appreciate the delicious simplicity of Japanese cuisine.

Ingredients:

- 1 lb thinly sliced beef (sirloin or ribeye)
- 1 onion, thinly sliced
- 2 cups cooked Japanese rice
- 2 tablespoons vegetable oil
- 2 tablespoons soy sauce
- 2 tablespoons mirin
- 2 tablespoons sake
- 1 tablespoon sugar
- 1 cup dashi stock
- Chopped green onions for garnish
- Pickled red ginger (beni shoga) for garnish (optional)

Instructions:

Prepare Dashi Stock:
- In a bowl, mix together soy sauce, mirin, sake, sugar, and dashi stock to create the broth.

Cook Beef and Onions:
- Heat vegetable oil in a pan over medium heat.
- Add thinly sliced onions and sauté until they become translucent.
- Add the thinly sliced beef to the pan and cook until browned.

Simmer in Broth:
- Pour the prepared broth over the beef and onions in the pan.
- Allow the mixture to simmer for a few minutes until the beef is fully cooked and the flavors meld.

Serve Over Rice:
- Place a serving of cooked Japanese rice in individual bowls.
- Spoon the simmered beef and onions over the rice.

Garnish:
- Garnish Gyu Don with chopped green onions and pickled red ginger (if using).

Serve Hot:
- Serve Gyu Don hot and enjoy the comforting and savory combination of beef, onions, and flavorful broth over rice.

Gyu Don is a classic Japanese comfort dish that offers a perfect balance of savory and sweet flavors. The thinly sliced beef, tenderized in a delectable broth, makes for a satisfying and delicious meal that can be enjoyed any day of the week.

Tamago Sando - Japanese Egg Salad Sandwich

Introduction:

Experience the simple yet delightful flavors of Tamago Sando, a Japanese egg salad sandwich that showcases the creaminess of seasoned eggs between slices of soft, pillowy bread. Enjoy this classic Japanese sandwich as a light and satisfying meal or snack.

Ingredients:

For Tamago (Egg Salad):

- 4 large eggs
- 2 tablespoons Japanese mayonnaise
- 1 teaspoon soy sauce
- 1 teaspoon mirin
- Salt and pepper to taste
- Chopped chives or green onions for garnish (optional)

For Assembly:

- Soft, white bread slices
- Butter for spreading (optional)
- Japanese mustard (optional)

Instructions:

Boil Eggs:
- Place the eggs in a saucepan and cover them with water.
- Bring the water to a boil, then reduce the heat and simmer for about 10 minutes.
- Transfer the boiled eggs to an ice bath to cool.

Prepare Tamago Filling:
- Peel the cooled eggs and finely chop them.
- In a bowl, combine chopped eggs, Japanese mayonnaise, soy sauce, mirin, salt, and pepper.
- Mix the ingredients until well combined. Adjust seasoning to taste.

Assemble Tamago Sando:
- If desired, lightly butter the slices of soft, white bread.

- Spoon a generous portion of the tamago filling onto one slice of bread.
- Optionally, add a small amount of Japanese mustard for extra flavor.
- Top with another slice of bread to create a sandwich.

Cut and Garnish:
- Trim the crusts off the sandwich if preferred.
- Cut the Tamago Sando into halves or quarters.
- Optionally, garnish with chopped chives or green onions for a fresh touch.

Serve:
- Serve Tamago Sando as a delightful and satisfying Japanese egg salad sandwich.

Tamago Sando is a beloved Japanese sandwich that features the creamy goodness of seasoned eggs. Its simplicity and comforting flavors make it a popular choice for a quick and tasty meal.

Hōtō - Japanese Pumpkin and Noodle Stew

Introduction:

Warm up with the comforting flavors of Hōtō, a traditional Japanese stew featuring thick wheat noodles, pumpkin, and a rich miso-based broth. This hearty and nutritious dish is perfect for colder days, offering a satisfying blend of textures and flavors.

Ingredients:

- 8 oz hōtō noodles (or substitute with udon noodles)
- 2 cups pumpkin, peeled and cut into bite-sized pieces
- 1 onion, sliced
- 2 carrots, sliced
- 2 cups spinach, chopped
- 4 cups dashi stock
- 3 tablespoons white miso paste
- 2 tablespoons soy sauce
- 1 tablespoon mirin
- 1 tablespoon vegetable oil
- Green onions, sliced, for garnish

Instructions:

Prepare Vegetables:
- Peel and cut the pumpkin into bite-sized pieces.
- Slice the onion and carrots.
- Chop the spinach.

Cook Vegetables:
- In a large pot, heat vegetable oil over medium heat.
- Add sliced onion and cook until softened.
- Add pumpkin and carrots to the pot and sauté for a few minutes.

Make Dashi Broth:
- Pour dashi stock into the pot with vegetables.
- In a small bowl, mix miso paste with a ladle of the hot broth until smooth. Add this miso mixture back to the pot.

Add Noodles:
- Add hōtō noodles (or udon noodles) to the pot and cook according to package instructions.

Season with Soy Sauce and Mirin:
- Add soy sauce and mirin to the pot. Stir well to combine.
- Let the stew simmer until the noodles are cooked and the vegetables are tender.

Add Spinach:
- Add chopped spinach to the pot and stir until wilted.

Garnish and Serve:
- Ladle the Hōtō into serving bowls.
- Garnish with sliced green onions.

Enjoy:
- Serve Hōtō hot and savor the comforting blend of noodles, vegetables, and miso broth.

Hōtō is a delightful Japanese stew that brings together the goodness of hearty noodles, pumpkin, and a flavorful miso-based broth. It's a wholesome and nourishing dish that captures the essence of home-cooked comfort.

Okonomiyaki - Japanese Savory Pancake

Introduction:

Embark on a culinary adventure with Okonomiyaki, a savory Japanese pancake that's customizable to your liking. Packed with shredded cabbage, meats, and other delicious ingredients, Okonomiyaki is cooked on a griddle and topped with a sweet and savory okonomiyaki sauce, mayo, and bonito flakes.

Ingredients:

For Okonomiyaki Batter:

- 2 cups shredded cabbage
- 1 cup all-purpose flour
- 2/3 cup dashi stock
- 2 large eggs
- 1 teaspoon soy sauce
- Salt and pepper to taste
- 1 cup additional ingredients (choose from sliced pork, shrimp, squid, green onions, etc.)

For Toppings and Sauce:

- Okonomiyaki sauce (store-bought or homemade with soy sauce, ketchup, Worcestershire sauce, and sugar)
- Japanese mayo
- Bonito flakes (katsuobushi)
- Aonori (seaweed flakes)

Instructions:

Prepare Batter:
- In a large bowl, combine shredded cabbage, all-purpose flour, dashi stock, eggs, soy sauce, salt, and pepper. Mix until well combined.
- Add your choice of additional ingredients (sliced pork, shrimp, etc.) and fold them into the batter.

Cook Okonomiyaki:
- Heat a griddle or non-stick pan over medium heat.

- Spoon the batter onto the griddle, forming a round pancake about 1/2 to 3/4 inch thick.
- Cook until the edges become golden brown, then flip the Okonomiyaki and cook the other side.

Finish Cooking:
- Continue cooking until both sides are golden brown and the center is cooked through. The total cooking time is around 8-10 minutes.

Top and Sauce:
- Transfer the cooked Okonomiyaki to a serving plate.
- Drizzle okonomiyaki sauce and Japanese mayo over the top in a zigzag pattern.

Garnish:
- Sprinkle bonito flakes and aonori (seaweed flakes) generously over the sauce.

Serve Hot:
- Serve Okonomiyaki hot, either whole on a plate or cut into wedges.

Enjoy:
- Enjoy the delightful mix of flavors and textures in this savory Japanese pancake.

Okonomiyaki is a versatile and fun dish that allows you to create your own flavor combinations. Whether you prefer it with meat, seafood, or vegetarian, Okonomiyaki is a tasty and satisfying addition to your Japanese culinary repertoire.

Zaru Soba - Japanese Cold Buckwheat Noodles

Introduction:

Cool down on a hot day with Zaru Soba, a refreshing and simple Japanese dish featuring cold buckwheat noodles served with a dipping sauce. This dish is not only delicious but also a perfect way to enjoy the unique texture and earthy flavor of soba noodles.

Ingredients:

For Soba Noodles:

- 8 oz soba noodles
- Ice water (for rinsing)

For Dipping Sauce (Tsuyu):

- 1/2 cup soy sauce
- 1/2 cup mirin
- 2 cups dashi stock
- 1 tablespoon sugar
- Wasabi (optional, for serving)

For Garnish (Optional):

- Nori (seaweed) strips
- Grated daikon radish
- Chopped green onions

Instructions:

Cook Soba Noodles:
- Boil soba noodles according to package instructions (usually around 4-5 minutes).
- Drain and rinse the noodles under cold running water to remove excess starch.
- Transfer the rinsed noodles to a bowl of ice water to cool completely.

Prepare Dipping Sauce (Tsuyu):
- In a saucepan, combine soy sauce, mirin, dashi stock, and sugar.

- Bring the mixture to a simmer over medium heat, stirring until the sugar dissolves.
- Remove from heat and let the dipping sauce cool.

Serve Zaru Soba:
- Drain the chilled soba noodles well.
- Arrange the soba noodles on a bamboo or mesh sieve (zaru) for individual servings.

Garnish (Optional):
- Optionally, garnish with nori strips, grated daikon radish, and chopped green onions.

Serve with Dipping Sauce:
- Serve Zaru Soba with individual bowls of dipping sauce.
- Optionally, add a small amount of wasabi to the dipping sauce for extra heat.

Enjoy:
- Dip the cold soba noodles into the dipping sauce and enjoy the refreshing taste of Zaru Soba.

Zaru Soba is a light and cooling dish that's perfect for hot weather. The combination of the nutty buckwheat noodles with the savory dipping sauce creates a delightful and satisfying culinary experience.

Miso Soup with Tofu and Wakame

Introduction:

Warm up with the comforting and umami-rich flavors of Miso Soup. This classic Japanese soup features a savory broth made with miso paste, tofu cubes, and tender wakame seaweed. It's a nourishing and soul-soothing dish that can be enjoyed as a starter or a light meal.

Ingredients:

- 4 cups dashi stock
- 3 tablespoons white miso paste
- 1/2 cup cubed tofu (silken or firm)
- 2 tablespoons dried wakame seaweed, rehydrated
- 2 green onions, thinly sliced
- 1 tablespoon soy sauce (optional)
- 1 teaspoon mirin (optional)
- Sliced shiitake mushrooms (optional)
- Grated ginger (optional)

Instructions:

Prepare Dashi Stock:
- In a pot, heat 4 cups of dashi stock over medium heat. If using instant dashi powder, follow the package instructions.

Dissolve Miso Paste:
- In a small bowl, dissolve the white miso paste in a ladleful of the hot dashi stock. Stir until smooth.

Add Miso Paste to Stock:
- Pour the dissolved miso paste back into the pot of dashi stock. Stir well to combine.

Add Tofu and Wakame:
- Add cubed tofu and rehydrated wakame seaweed to the pot.
- Optionally, add sliced shiitake mushrooms for added flavor.

Season (Optional):
- Add soy sauce and mirin to the soup, adjusting the quantities to taste.
- Optionally, add a small amount of grated ginger for a hint of freshness.

Simmer Gently:

- Allow the soup to simmer gently for a few minutes until the tofu is heated through and the wakame is tender.

Garnish:
- Garnish the miso soup with thinly sliced green onions.

Serve Hot:
- Ladle the hot miso soup into bowls and serve immediately.

Miso Soup with Tofu and Wakame is a classic and comforting Japanese dish that warms both the body and the soul. The combination of miso paste, tofu, and seaweed creates a harmonious and satisfying flavor profile that's perfect for any occasion.

Nikujaga - Japanese Meat and Potato Stew

Introduction:

Savor the hearty and comforting flavors of Nikujaga, a classic Japanese stew that combines tender beef, potatoes, and vegetables in a savory-sweet soy-based broth. This one-pot dish is a staple in Japanese home cooking, offering a perfect balance of protein and vegetables.

Ingredients:

- 1 lb thinly sliced beef (sukiyaki or stew beef)
- 4 medium potatoes, peeled and cut into bite-sized chunks
- 2 carrots, sliced into rounds
- 1 onion, thinly sliced
- 1 cup green beans, cut into bite-sized pieces
- 2 cups dashi stock
- 1/4 cup soy sauce
- 3 tablespoons mirin
- 2 tablespoons sugar
- 2 tablespoons vegetable oil
- 1 tablespoon sake (optional)
- Salt and pepper to taste
- Chopped green onions for garnish

Instructions:

Prepare Vegetables:
- Peel and cut the potatoes into bite-sized chunks.
- Slice the carrots into rounds.
- Thinly slice the onion.
- Cut green beans into bite-sized pieces.

Cook Beef:
- In a large pot, heat vegetable oil over medium heat.
- Add thinly sliced beef and cook until browned.

Add Vegetables:
- Add sliced onion, potatoes, carrots, and green beans to the pot. Sauté for a few minutes until the vegetables are slightly tender.

Make Dashi Broth:

- Pour dashi stock into the pot with vegetables and beef.

Season with Soy Sauce, Mirin, and Sugar:
- Add soy sauce, mirin, sugar, and sake (if using) to the pot. Stir well to combine.
- Season with salt and pepper to taste.

Simmer:
- Bring the mixture to a boil, then reduce the heat to low.
- Cover the pot and let the stew simmer until the potatoes are fully cooked and the flavors meld.

Garnish:
- Garnish Nikujaga with chopped green onions.

Serve Hot:
- Ladle the hot Nikujaga into bowls and serve with steamed rice.

Nikujaga is a wholesome and flavorful Japanese stew that reflects the comfort and warmth of home-cooked meals. The combination of beef, potatoes, and vegetables in a savory-sweet broth makes it a favorite among families in Japan.

Goma-ae - Japanese Sesame Spinach Salad

Introduction:

Enjoy the delightful simplicity of Goma-ae, a Japanese side dish that features blanched spinach dressed in a sweet and savory sesame sauce. This easy-to-make salad showcases the nutty flavor of sesame seeds, creating a perfect balance with the tender spinach leaves.

Ingredients:

- 1 bunch spinach, washed and trimmed
- 2 tablespoons sesame seeds
- 1 tablespoon soy sauce
- 1 tablespoon mirin
- 1 tablespoon sugar
- 1 teaspoon sesame oil

Instructions:

Blanch Spinach:
- Bring a pot of water to a boil.
- Add a pinch of salt to the boiling water.
- Blanch the spinach in the boiling water for about 1-2 minutes or until just wilted.

Shock in Ice Water:
- Quickly transfer the blanched spinach to a bowl of ice water to stop the cooking process.
- Drain and squeeze excess water from the spinach.

Prepare Sesame Sauce:
- In a small pan, toast sesame seeds over medium heat until fragrant. Be careful not to burn them.
- Grind the toasted sesame seeds using a mortar and pestle or a grinder until coarsely ground.

Make Sesame Sauce:
- In a bowl, combine the ground sesame seeds, soy sauce, mirin, sugar, and sesame oil. Mix well until the sugar is dissolved.

Dress Spinach:
- Place the blanched and drained spinach in a serving bowl.

- Pour the sesame sauce over the spinach and toss gently to coat the leaves evenly.

Chill (Optional):
- You can chill the Goma-ae in the refrigerator for a short time if you prefer a cold salad.

Serve:
- Serve Goma-ae as a refreshing side dish or part of a traditional Japanese meal.

Goma-ae is a light and flavorful way to enjoy spinach, and its nutty sesame dressing adds a distinctive touch to the dish. This classic Japanese salad is both healthy and delicious, making it a popular choice for those who appreciate the simplicity of Japanese cuisine.

Ebi Chili - Japanese Spicy Chili Prawns

Introduction:

Spice up your meal with Ebi Chili, a delectable Japanese dish featuring succulent prawns coated in a sweet and spicy chili sauce. This flavorful and visually appealing dish is perfect as an appetizer or as part of a vibrant Japanese spread.

Ingredients:

- 1 lb large prawns, peeled and deveined
- 1/2 cup cornstarch (for coating prawns)
- Vegetable oil for frying

For Chili Sauce:

- 2 tablespoons vegetable oil
- 3 cloves garlic, minced
- 1 tablespoon ginger, minced
- 2 tablespoons soy sauce
- 2 tablespoons ketchup
- 1 tablespoon sweet chili sauce
- 1 tablespoon oyster sauce
- 1 tablespoon sugar
- 1 teaspoon sesame oil
- Red chili flakes or sliced red chili (adjust to taste)
- Chopped green onions for garnish

Instructions:

Coat and Fry Prawns:
- Pat dry the prawns with paper towels.
- Coat the prawns in cornstarch, shaking off any excess.
- Heat vegetable oil in a pan for frying. Fry the prawns until golden brown and crispy. Set aside.

Make Chili Sauce:

- In a separate pan, heat vegetable oil over medium heat.
- Add minced garlic and ginger. Sauté until fragrant.

Prepare Chili Sauce:
- Add soy sauce, ketchup, sweet chili sauce, oyster sauce, sugar, sesame oil, and red chili flakes (or sliced red chili) to the pan. Stir well to combine.

Coat Prawns in Sauce:
- Once the sauce is well combined and heated through, add the fried prawns to the pan.
- Toss the prawns in the chili sauce, ensuring they are evenly coated.

Garnish and Serve:
- Transfer the Ebi Chili to a serving plate.
- Garnish with chopped green onions for a fresh touch.

Serve Hot:
- Serve Ebi Chili hot as a flavorful and spicy appetizer.

Ebi Chili is a mouthwatering Japanese dish that combines the succulence of prawns with a sweet and spicy chili sauce. It's a crowd-pleaser and a great addition to your repertoire of Japanese-inspired recipes.

Chawanmushi - Japanese Steamed Egg Custard

Introduction:

Delight in the delicate and silky texture of Chawanmushi, a traditional Japanese steamed egg custard. This savory custard is filled with a medley of ingredients such as chicken, shrimp, mushrooms, and ginkgo nuts, creating a harmonious blend of flavors in every spoonful.

Ingredients:

- 3 large eggs
- 2 cups dashi stock
- 1 tablespoon soy sauce
- 1 tablespoon mirin
- 1/2 teaspoon salt
- 1/2 teaspoon sugar
- 1/2 cup chicken breast, thinly sliced
- 1/2 cup shrimp, peeled and deveined
- 1/2 cup shiitake mushrooms, sliced
- 1/4 cup ginkgo nuts, peeled (optional)
- 1 green onion, thinly sliced
- Kamaboko (fish cake), thinly sliced (optional)

Instructions:

Prepare Dashi Stock:
- In a bowl, mix dashi stock, soy sauce, mirin, salt, and sugar. Stir until well combined.

Beat Eggs:
- In a separate bowl, beat the eggs until well blended.

Combine Eggs and Dashi Mixture:
- Slowly add the beaten eggs to the dashi mixture, stirring gently to avoid creating bubbles.

Prepare Ingredients:
- Thinly slice the chicken breast, peel and devein the shrimp, slice the shiitake mushrooms, and peel the ginkgo nuts (if using).

Assemble Chawanmushi:

- Divide the prepared ingredients evenly among individual chawanmushi cups or small heatproof bowls.
- Pour the egg and dashi mixture over the ingredients in each cup.

Steam:
- Steam the chawanmushi cups in a steamer over medium heat for about 15-20 minutes or until the custard is set.

Garnish:
- Once set, garnish each chawanmushi with sliced green onions and kamaboko (if using).

Serve Warm:
- Serve Chawanmushi warm and enjoy the velvety texture and savory goodness.

Chawanmushi is a comforting and elegant Japanese dish that showcases the art of steaming eggs to perfection. With its rich and savory custard, Chawanmushi is a delightful addition to any Japanese meal or as a standalone appetizer.

Buta Kakuni - Japanese Braised Pork Belly

Introduction:

Indulge in the rich and flavorful Buta Kakuni, a Japanese dish that features melt-in-your-mouth braised pork belly simmered in a sweet and savory soy-based broth. This classic dish is a true comfort food, showcasing the art of slow-cooking to achieve tender and succulent pork.

Ingredients:

- 2 lbs pork belly, cut into large cubes
- 1 cup sake
- 1 cup mirin
- 1 cup soy sauce
- 1 cup water
- 1 cup sugar
- 4 slices ginger
- 4 cloves garlic, crushed
- 2 green onions, cut into large pieces
- 1 tablespoon vegetable oil

Instructions:

Prepare Pork Belly:
- Cut the pork belly into large cubes, removing excess skin if desired.

Sear Pork Belly:
- In a large pot or Dutch oven, heat vegetable oil over medium-high heat.
- Sear the pork belly cubes on all sides until browned. This enhances the flavor of the meat.

Prepare Braising Liquid:
- In a bowl, mix together sake, mirin, soy sauce, water, and sugar.

Braise Pork Belly:
- Add ginger slices, crushed garlic, and green onions to the pot with the seared pork belly.
- Pour the braising liquid over the pork belly.

Simmer:
- Bring the mixture to a boil, then reduce the heat to low.
- Cover the pot and let the pork belly simmer for 2 to 2.5 hours or until the meat is tender and easily pierced with a fork.

Serve:
- Once the pork belly is tender, remove it from the pot and arrange it on a serving plate.

Reduce Sauce (Optional):
- If desired, you can further reduce the braising liquid to a thicker consistency by simmering it over medium heat.

Garnish and Serve:
- Pour the reduced sauce over the pork belly.
- Garnish with sliced green onions or other preferred toppings.

Serve Hot:
- Serve Buta Kakuni hot with steamed rice or as part of a traditional Japanese meal.

Buta Kakuni is a sumptuous and savory dish that beautifully combines the sweetness of mirin and sugar with the umami of soy sauce, resulting in a mouthwatering experience. Enjoy the tender and flavorful pork belly that has absorbed the rich broth during the slow braising process.

Nasu Dengaku - Japanese Miso-Glazed Eggplant

Introduction:

Savor the delightful combination of sweet and savory flavors with Nasu Dengaku, a classic Japanese dish featuring grilled eggplant coated in a glossy miso glaze. This dish is not only visually appealing but also a perfect balance of textures and tastes.

Ingredients:

- 2 large Japanese eggplants
- 2 tablespoons white miso paste
- 1 tablespoon mirin
- 1 tablespoon sake
- 2 tablespoons sugar
- Vegetable oil for brushing
- Sesame seeds and chopped green onions for garnish

Instructions:

Prepare Eggplants:
- Cut the eggplants in half lengthwise. Score the cut side of each eggplant with a crisscross pattern.

Preheat Grill or Oven:
- Preheat your grill or oven broiler.

Grill Eggplants:
- Brush the cut side of each eggplant with vegetable oil.
- Grill the eggplants, cut side down, until they are lightly charred and tender. Flip and cook the skin side briefly.

Make Miso Glaze:
- In a small saucepan, combine white miso paste, mirin, sake, and sugar.
- Heat the mixture over low heat, stirring continuously until the sugar dissolves and the miso is well incorporated.

Coat Eggplants with Miso Glaze:
- Brush the grilled side of each eggplant with the miso glaze.
- Place the glazed side under the grill or broiler for a few minutes until the glaze becomes glossy and caramelized.

Garnish:

- Sprinkle sesame seeds and chopped green onions over the glazed eggplants.

Serve Hot:
- Serve Nasu Dengaku hot as a flavorful appetizer or side dish.

Nasu Dengaku is a delicious way to enjoy the unique texture and flavor of Japanese eggplants. The miso glaze adds depth and richness to the dish, making it a favorite among those who appreciate the complexity of Japanese flavors.

Yudofu - Japanese Hot Tofu Soup

Introduction:

Experience the simplicity and purity of Yudofu, a traditional Japanese hot tofu soup that highlights the delicate flavors of tofu simmered in a light kombu (seaweed) broth. This dish embodies the essence of Japanese cuisine, allowing the natural goodness of tofu to shine.

Ingredients:

- 1 block (about 14 oz) silken tofu, cut into bite-sized cubes
- 4 cups kombu (seaweed) dashi stock
- 2 tablespoons soy sauce
- 1 tablespoon mirin
- 2 green onions, thinly sliced
- Grated ginger for garnish (optional)

Instructions:

Prepare Kombu Dashi Stock:
- In a pot, steep kombu in 4 cups of water for at least 30 minutes to create kombu dashi stock.

Simmer Tofu in Dashi:
- Gently bring the kombu dashi stock to a simmer over low to medium heat.
- Add the bite-sized tofu cubes to the simmering dashi.

Season with Soy Sauce and Mirin:
- Stir in soy sauce and mirin, ensuring an even distribution of flavors.

Simmer Gently:
- Allow the tofu to simmer gently in the dashi for about 10-15 minutes. Be careful not to stir too vigorously to maintain the tofu's delicate texture.

Garnish:
- Garnish Yudofu with thinly sliced green onions and, if desired, a sprinkle of grated ginger.

Serve Hot:
- Ladle the hot Yudofu into individual bowls and serve immediately.

Enjoy the Simplicity:
- Savor the pure and delicate flavors of Yudofu, appreciating the subtle taste of silken tofu in a light kombu dashi broth.

Yudofu is a celebration of simplicity, allowing the natural flavors of tofu to take center stage. This Japanese hot tofu soup is not only nourishing but also a soothing and gentle dish that reflects the culinary elegance of Japanese cuisine.

Unagi Don - Japanese Grilled Eel Rice Bowl

Introduction:

Indulge in the rich and savory goodness of Unagi Don, a classic Japanese dish featuring grilled eel glazed with a sweet soy-based sauce, served over a bed of steamed rice. This delectable rice bowl is a true delicacy that captures the essence of traditional Japanese flavors.

Ingredients:

- 2 unagi (freshwater eel) fillets, deboned
- 1/2 cup soy sauce
- 1/4 cup mirin
- 2 tablespoons sake
- 2 tablespoons sugar
- 2 cups steamed Japanese rice
- Nori (seaweed) strips for garnish
- Toasted sesame seeds for garnish
- Chopped green onions for garnish

Instructions:

Prepare Unagi Fillets:
- If the unagi fillets are frozen, thaw them according to package instructions.
- Score the skin side of the unagi fillets diagonally to allow the sauce to penetrate.

Make Unagi Sauce:
- In a saucepan, combine soy sauce, mirin, sake, and sugar.
- Heat the mixture over low heat, stirring until the sugar dissolves. Simmer for a few minutes to allow the flavors to meld.

Grill Unagi:
- Preheat your grill or broiler.
- Grill the scored side of the unagi fillets first, basting with the sauce.
- Flip the fillets and continue grilling until the skin is crispy and the eel is fully cooked, basting with the sauce.

Glaze with Sauce:

- Brush the unagi fillets generously with the sauce, ensuring they are well coated.

Prepare Rice:
- Steam Japanese rice and divide it into serving bowls.

Assemble Unagi Don:
- Place the grilled unagi fillets on top of the steamed rice in each bowl.

Garnish:
- Garnish Unagi Don with nori strips, toasted sesame seeds, and chopped green onions.

Serve Hot:
- Serve Unagi Don hot and savor the exquisite flavors of grilled eel over perfectly steamed rice.

Unagi Don is a luxurious and satisfying dish that combines the smoky, sweet, and savory notes of grilled eel with the simplicity of steamed rice. This Japanese rice bowl is a treat for those who appreciate the indulgence of traditional flavors.

Dorayaki - Japanese Red Bean Pancake Sandwiches

Introduction:

Treat yourself to the sweet and fluffy goodness of Dorayaki, a popular Japanese confection that features two pancake-like cakes filled with sweet red bean paste. This delightful dessert is not only delicious but also a nostalgic favorite enjoyed by many.

Ingredients:

For Dorayaki Batter:

- 2 large eggs
- 1/2 cup sugar
- 1 tablespoon honey
- 1 cup all-purpose flour
- 1 teaspoon baking powder
- 1/2 cup water

For Red Bean Paste Filling:

- 1 cup sweetened red bean paste (store-bought or homemade)

Instructions:

    Make Dorayaki Batter:
- In a bowl, beat eggs and sugar together until well combined and slightly frothy.
- Add honey to the egg mixture and mix well.

Sift Dry Ingredients:
- In a separate bowl, sift together all-purpose flour and baking powder.

Combine Wet and Dry Ingredients:
- Gradually add the sifted dry ingredients to the egg mixture, stirring continuously to avoid lumps.
- Add water to the batter and mix until smooth.

Rest the Batter:
- Let the batter rest for about 15-20 minutes to allow it to slightly thicken.

Cook Dorayaki Pancakes:
- Heat a non-stick pan or griddle over medium heat.

- Spoon small portions of the batter onto the pan to form pancakes. Cook until bubbles appear on the surface, then flip and cook the other side until golden brown.

Assemble Dorayaki:
- Once the pancakes are cooked, spread a spoonful of sweetened red bean paste on one pancake.
- Place another pancake on top, creating a sandwich.

Serve Warm or Cold:
- Serve Dorayaki warm or at room temperature.

Enjoy:
- Enjoy the delightful combination of soft, fluffy pancakes and sweet red bean paste in these classic Japanese confections.

Dorayaki is a beloved sweet treat in Japan, often enjoyed with a cup of tea or as a delightful snack. The contrast of the tender pancakes with the sweet red bean filling makes Dorayaki a perfect indulgence for those with a sweet tooth.

Takoyaki - Japanese Octopus Balls

Introduction:

Experience the fun and flavorful world of Takoyaki, a popular street food in Japan. These savory octopus balls are made with a batter filled with tender octopus pieces, green onions, and pickled ginger, then topped with takoyaki sauce, mayo, bonito flakes, and seaweed. Get ready to enjoy the deliciousness of these bite-sized delights!

Ingredients:

For Takoyaki Batter:

- 2 cups takoyaki flour (or a mixture of all-purpose flour and dashi stock)
- 2 1/2 cups water
- 2 eggs
- 1/2 teaspoon soy sauce
- 1/2 teaspoon mirin
- 1/2 teaspoon salt

For Filling:

- 1 cup cooked octopus, diced into small pieces
- 4 green onions, finely chopped
- 2 tablespoons pickled red ginger (beni shoga), finely chopped

For Toppings:

- Takoyaki sauce
- Japanese mayonnaise
- Bonito flakes (katsuobushi)
- Aonori (seaweed flakes)

Instructions:

   Prepare Batter:
   - In a large bowl, whisk together takoyaki flour, water, eggs, soy sauce, mirin, and salt until you achieve a smooth batter.

   Heat Takoyaki Pan:

- Heat a takoyaki pan on medium heat and brush the cavities with oil or use a non-stick takoyaki pan.

Pour Batter into Cavities:
- Pour the batter into the cavities of the takoyaki pan, filling each one almost to the top.

Add Filling:
- Add diced octopus, chopped green onions, and pickled red ginger into each takoyaki cavity.

Cook and Flip:
- Allow the batter to cook for a minute or so until the edges start to set.
- Using a takoyaki pick or skewer, flip each takoyaki ball to cook the other side until golden brown and crispy.

Form Round Shape:
- Continue rotating the takoyaki balls in the cavities until they form a round shape.

Serve and Top:
- Transfer the takoyaki to a plate.
- Drizzle takoyaki sauce and Japanese mayo over the top.
- Sprinkle bonito flakes and aonori generously.

Serve Hot:
- Serve Takoyaki hot and enjoy these flavorful octopus balls!

Takoyaki is a delightful and iconic Japanese street food that brings joy with every bite. The combination of the tender octopus, savory batter, and umami-rich toppings makes it a must-try for anyone exploring Japanese cuisine.

Okonomiyaki - Japanese Savory Pancake

Introduction:

Okonomiyaki, often referred to as a Japanese savory pancake or "Japanese pizza," is a versatile and customizable dish that combines a flavorful batter with various ingredients. Enjoy the delicious medley of shredded cabbage, meats, seafood, and other ingredients, topped with okonomiyaki sauce and mayonnaise.

Ingredients:

For Okonomiyaki Batter:

- 2 cups all-purpose flour
- 1 1/2 cups dashi stock
- 2 large eggs
- 1/2 teaspoon salt
- 1/2 teaspoon soy sauce

For Okonomiyaki Filling:

- 3 cups shredded cabbage
- 1 cup sliced green onions
- 1/2 cup tenkasu (tempura crumbs)
- 1/2 cup cooked protein (chopped cooked shrimp, squid, pork, or a combination)
- Optional: 1/4 cup pickled red ginger (beni shoga)

For Cooking:

- Vegetable oil for cooking

For Topping:

- Okonomiyaki sauce
- Japanese mayonnaise
- Bonito flakes (katsuobushi)
- Aonori (seaweed flakes)

Instructions:

Prepare Okonomiyaki Batter:
- In a large bowl, whisk together all-purpose flour, dashi stock, eggs, salt, and soy sauce until smooth.

Prepare Okonomiyaki Filling:
- Add shredded cabbage, sliced green onions, tenkasu, cooked protein, and pickled red ginger (if using) to the batter. Mix well to combine.

Cook Okonomiyaki:
- Heat vegetable oil in a large skillet or griddle over medium heat.
- Pour a portion of the batter onto the hot skillet to form a round pancake, about 6-8 inches in diameter.

Cook Both Sides:
- Cook the okonomiyaki for about 4-5 minutes on each side or until golden brown and cooked through.

Top and Serve:
- Drizzle okonomiyaki sauce and Japanese mayo over the top of the cooked pancake.
- Sprinkle bonito flakes and aonori generously.

Serve Hot:
- Serve Okonomiyaki hot, either whole or sliced into wedges.

Okonomiyaki is a crowd-pleasing dish that allows for creativity in choosing ingredients. Whether you prefer seafood, meat, or a vegetarian option, Okonomiyaki is a delightful and customizable addition to your Japanese cuisine repertoire.

Sakura Soba Noodles with Tempura Vegetables

Ingredients:

For Sakura Soba Noodles:

- 250g Sakura soba noodles
- 4 cups dashi broth
- 1/4 cup soy sauce
- 2 tablespoons mirin
- 1 tablespoon sake
- 1 teaspoon sugar
- 1 cup thinly sliced green onions (for garnish)
- 1 cup sakura (cherry blossom) petals (edible, for garnish)

For Tempura Vegetables:

- Assorted vegetables (sweet potato, zucchini, broccoli florets, bell peppers)
- 1 cup all-purpose flour
- 1 cup ice-cold water
- 1 egg
- Vegetable oil for frying

Instructions:

Cook the Sakura Soba Noodles:
a. Cook the soba noodles according to the package instructions.
b. In a separate pot, combine dashi broth, soy sauce, mirin, sake, and sugar. Bring to a simmer.

c. Drain the soba noodles and add them to the simmering broth. Cook for an additional 2-3 minutes until heated through.

Prepare Tempura Batter:
a. In a bowl, whisk together flour, ice-cold water, and egg until the batter is smooth.

b. Heat vegetable oil in a deep fryer or a large, deep pan to 350°F (180°C).

Make Tempura Vegetables:
a. Dip assorted vegetables into the tempura batter, ensuring they are fully coated.

b. Carefully place the coated vegetables into the hot oil and fry until golden brown. Remove and drain on paper towels.

Assemble the Dish:
a. Divide the Sakura soba noodles among serving bowls.
b. Top with a variety of tempura vegetables.

c. Garnish with thinly sliced green onions and edible sakura petals.

Serve:

a. Serve the Sakura Soba Noodles with Tempura Vegetables hot, accompanied by soy sauce and wasabi if desired.

This Japanese-inspired dish combines the delicate flavors of Sakura soba noodles with the crispy goodness of tempura vegetables, creating a harmonious and visually stunning meal that captures the essence of Japanese cuisine.

Miso Glazed Grilled Salmon with Sake-infused Jasmine Rice

Ingredients:

For Miso Glazed Grilled Salmon:

- 4 salmon fillets
- 1/4 cup white miso paste
- 2 tablespoons mirin
- 2 tablespoons sake
- 2 tablespoons soy sauce
- 1 tablespoon honey
- 1 teaspoon grated fresh ginger
- 2 cloves garlic, minced
- Sesame seeds for garnish
- Sliced green onions for garnish

For Sake-infused Jasmine Rice:

- 1 cup jasmine rice
- 1 1/2 cups water
- 1/4 cup sake
- 1 tablespoon soy sauce
- 1 tablespoon rice vinegar
- 1 teaspoon sugar

For Pickled Cucumber Salad:

- 1 cucumber, thinly sliced
- 1/4 cup rice vinegar
- 1 tablespoon sugar
- 1/2 teaspoon salt
- Red pepper flakes for a hint of spice

Instructions:

Prepare Miso Glazed Grilled Salmon:

a. In a bowl, whisk together miso paste, mirin, sake, soy sauce, honey, grated ginger, and minced garlic.

b. Marinate the salmon fillets in the mixture for at least 30 minutes.

c. Preheat the grill to medium-high heat. Grill the salmon for 4-5 minutes per side, or until cooked to your liking.

d. Baste the salmon with the marinade during grilling. Sprinkle sesame seeds and sliced green onions for garnish.

Cook Sake-infused Jasmine Rice:

a. Rinse jasmine rice under cold water until the water runs clear.

b. In a rice cooker, combine rice, water, sake, soy sauce, rice vinegar, and sugar. Cook according to the rice cooker instructions.

Make Pickled Cucumber Salad:

a. In a bowl, mix rice vinegar, sugar, salt, and red pepper flakes until sugar and salt dissolve.

b. Add thinly sliced cucumbers to the mixture and toss to coat. Allow it to marinate for at least 15 minutes.

Assemble the Dish:

a. Serve the Miso Glazed Grilled Salmon on a bed of sake-infused jasmine rice.

b. Garnish with pickled cucumber salad on the side.

Enjoy this delightful Japanese-inspired dish with the unique combination of flavors from the miso-glazed salmon, sake-infused jasmine rice, and refreshing pickled cucumber salad.

Teriyaki Tofu Stir-Fry with Udon Noodles

Ingredients:

For Teriyaki Tofu:

- 1 block firm tofu, pressed and cubed
- 1/4 cup soy sauce
- 2 tablespoons mirin
- 1 tablespoon sake
- 2 tablespoons brown sugar
- 1 teaspoon grated fresh ginger
- 2 cloves garlic, minced
- 1 tablespoon vegetable oil

For Udon Noodles Stir-Fry:

- 8 oz udon noodles, cooked according to package instructions
- 1 cup broccoli florets
- 1 bell pepper, thinly sliced
- 1 carrot, julienned
- 1 cup snow peas, trimmed
- 2 tablespoons vegetable oil
- Sesame seeds for garnish
- Sliced green onions for garnish

Instructions:

Prepare Teriyaki Tofu:
a. In a bowl, whisk together soy sauce, mirin, sake, brown sugar, grated ginger, and minced garlic to make the teriyaki sauce.
b. Heat vegetable oil in a pan over medium-high heat. Add cubed tofu and cook until golden brown on all sides.

c. Pour the teriyaki sauce over the tofu, coating it evenly. Cook for an additional 2-3 minutes until the sauce thickens.

Cook Udon Noodles Stir-Fry:
a. In a large wok or skillet, heat vegetable oil over medium-high heat.
b. Add broccoli, bell pepper, carrot, and snow peas. Stir-fry for 3-4 minutes until the vegetables are tender-crisp.

    c. Add cooked udon noodles to the vegetables and toss until well combined.

Assemble the Dish:

a. Place the teriyaki tofu on top of the udon noodles and vegetables.

    b. Garnish with sesame seeds and sliced green onions.

Serve this Teriyaki Tofu Stir-Fry with Udon Noodles hot, enjoying the savory teriyaki flavor paired with the chewy udon noodles and crisp vegetables.

Optional: Add a dash of sriracha or chili oil for some extra heat if desired.

Matcha Green Tea Pancakes with Red Bean Paste Drizzle

Ingredients:

For Matcha Green Tea Pancakes:

- 1 cup all-purpose flour
- 2 tablespoons matcha green tea powder
- 2 tablespoons sugar
- 1 teaspoon baking powder
- 1/2 teaspoon baking soda
- Pinch of salt
- 3/4 cup buttermilk
- 1 large egg
- 2 tablespoons unsalted butter, melted
- 1 teaspoon vanilla extract

For Red Bean Paste Drizzle:

- 1/2 cup sweetened red bean paste
- 2 tablespoons water

For Garnish:

- Whipped cream
- Fresh strawberries, sliced

Instructions:

Make Matcha Green Tea Pancakes:
a. In a large bowl, whisk together flour, matcha powder, sugar, baking powder, baking soda, and salt.
b. In a separate bowl, whisk together buttermilk, egg, melted butter, and vanilla extract.
c. Pour the wet ingredients into the dry ingredients and gently fold until just combined. Do not overmix; a few lumps are okay.

    d. Heat a griddle or non-stick pan over medium heat. Pour 1/4 cup portions of batter onto the griddle and cook until bubbles form on the surface. Flip and cook until both sides are golden brown.

Prepare Red Bean Paste Drizzle:

a. In a small saucepan, heat red bean paste and water over low heat. Stir until the paste becomes a smooth, drizzle-like consistency.

Assemble the Dish:

a. Stack the Matcha Green Tea Pancakes on a serving plate.

b. Drizzle the warm red bean paste over the pancake stack.

   c. Garnish with whipped cream and sliced fresh strawberries.

Serve these delightful Matcha Green Tea Pancakes with Red Bean Paste Drizzle for a unique and delicious Japanese-inspired breakfast or dessert.

Optional: Dust the pancakes with a bit of extra matcha powder for an added burst of green tea flavor.